DEATH
in the midst of life

DEATH
in the midst of life

*Social and Cultural Influences
on Death, Grief, and Mourning*

JACK B. KAMERMAN

Kean College of New Jersey

Prentice Hall   Englewood Cliffs, New Jersey 07632

Library of Congress Cataloging-in-Publication Data

KAMERMAN, JACK B.
  Death in the midst of life.

  Bibliography: p.
  Includes index.
  1. Death—Social aspects—United States.
2. Grief. I. Title.
HQ1073.5.U6K35 1987   306   87-2321
ISBN 0-13-197708-3

Editorial/production
  supervision: Arthur Maisel
Cover design: Ben Santora

Printed in the United States of America

10 9 8 7 6 5 4

ISBN   0-13-197708-3   01

Prentice-Hall International (UK) Limited, *London*
Prentice-Hall of Australia Pty. Limited, *Sydney*
Prentice-Hall Canada Inc., *Toronto*
Prentice-Hall Hispanoamericana, S. A., *Mexico*
Prentice-Hall of India Private Limited, *New Delhi*
Prentice-Hall of Japan, Inc., *Tokyo*
Prentice-Hall of Southeast Asia Pte. Ltd., *Singapore*
Editora Prentice-Hall do Brasil, Ltda., *Rio de Janeiro*

To Connie,
who reminds me every day how
precious life is

CONTENTS

PREFACE

In 1963, I participated in a seminar on death given by Robert Fulton at the University of Minnesota. It was probably the first American university course in the sociology of death. A friend, Calvin Appleby, persuaded me to attend against what seemed at the time my better judgment. The few participants in the seminar had something of the feeling of pioneers. We soon learned not to discuss our work with friends nor to carry our textbooks too openly (particularly on airplanes).

Shortly afterward, Cal Appleby and I, with youthful presumption, taught a death course in the Free University of Minnesota, a nontraditional, nonaffiliated collection of noncredit classes, held in a building which was owned by a religious organization close to the University of Minnesota campus in Minneapolis.

In 1968, I developed and taught my own death course in the Sociology Department of Adelphi University in Garden City, New York. I subsequently developed and taught death courses at three other colleges and universities in the New York metropolitan area.

One thing that struck me over that period was the relative scarcity of textbooks on death written from a sociological point of view. In the courses I've taught, I have had to use sociological monographs and nominally multidisciplinary (but in fact heavily psychologistic) texts and readers.

What I have tried to do is write a brief book on death from a consistently sociological perspective. It is intended for use in undergraduate sociology courses on death as well as death courses offered in other programs, e.g., psychology, nursing, social work, and health education—courses that have until now been dominated by texts with a psychologistic bias. The book can be used by itself or in conjunction with readers or monographs.

While the book is an attempt to *understand* death, my experiences with students for over twenty years have indicated that this approach also has great practical value in helping them cope with deaths they have encountered or will inevitably encounter. I have *tried* to steer a relatively value-neutral course through a decidedly emotion-laden area.

For the best in this book, I wish to thank Robert Fulton for introducing me to the sociological perspective on death, Calvin Appleby for introducing me to Robert Fulton and starting me out in death education, and the late Gregory P. Stone for grounding my thinking in symbolic interactionism. I owe Edwin S. Shneidman a great intellectual and personal debt for encouraging me to see a perspective beyond sociology and a professional life beyond this book.

I also wish to thank Raymond L. Schmitt of Illinois State University, Carol-Rae Green Hoffman of Montgomery County Community College, and Ricardo Joseph of Santa Rosa Junior College for their reviews of earlier drafts of the manuscript. I am particularly grateful to Ray Schmitt for his unerring intelligence and good sense. My students helped me to conceive this book, and my sabbatical from Kean College helped me to complete it. I owe thanks to Bill Webber, Kathleen Dorman, and Arthur Maisel of Prentice-Hall for their patience and good humor.

Last and most, I wish to thank Constance Munro, my wife, for editorial help, grace, optimism, and other gifts too numerous and wonderful to disserve with mere words.

Jack B. Kamerman

Thanks are due to the following publishers for kind permission to use material as indicated:

Excerpt from John P. Brantner, "Death and the Self," in *Death Education: Preparation for Living*, edited by Betty R. Green and Donald P. Irish. Reprinted by permission of Schenkman Publishing Company.
Excerpt from Jessica Mitford, *The American Way of Death*. Reprinted by permission of Simon and Schuster and the author.

CHAPTER ONE
INTRODUCTION: DEATH IN THE CONTEXT OF AMERICAN LIFE

In the midst of life we are in death.
-Book of Common Prayer

As much as we try, we cannot exorcize the world of death from the world of life. For one thing, death is an immutable fact of life. On different schedules, after postponing and denying with varying degrees of success, before the right time or after the right time (never, it seems, at precisely the right time), surrounded by loved ones or isolated by changing social patterns, we all die.

Because of the inevitability of death, keeping it hidden, even partially hidden, is an accomplishment rather than a natural feature of the world; that is, it says more about the way we see things than the way things "are." In the same way individuals expend enormous amounts of emotional energy to keep a painful personal experience out of their minds, mechanisms have developed in American society to keep death out of sight and out of minds. But just as blocking doesn't change the fact that these painful experiences have taken place, the avoidance and denial of death on a societal level doesn't change the fact that people still die, although later and less conspicuously.

Of course, the manner in which death is handled varies from culture to culture and from time to time. The attitudes and behaviors that accompany death and dying are products of particular cultures at particular times.

Although death was once a fixture of everyday life in America, it was banished from polite society during the course of this century. In the past twenty-five years, it has returned to public discussion, if not public life. In a sense, like the relative who, though uninvited to a family function "attends" anyway in the obsessive thoughts and compulsive conversation of those present, death seems to have returned. In fact, by its persistent presence and unavoidably conspicuous absence, death has remained in the midst of life.

THE RISE IN PUBLIC ATTENTION TO DEATH

Throughout the nineteenth century, death was conspicuous in American life. Death was framed by religion. In addition, people died at home more often than in hospitals. The family, sometimes aided by undertakers, prepared the body that was displayed at home. Signs of death were everywhere. Bodies were photographed for memorial purposes. Black crepe was hung on the outside door of a house in mourning. Mourning dress was worn, the fine gradations of mourning dress observed most often by the wealthier classes. Widows wore only clothing of muted black for the first year after their husbands' death. For the first half of the second year, shiny black was allowed, and in the remainder of that year, white and violet could be worn in addition. After two years, normal dress could again be worn; older widows, however, wore mourning for the rest of their lives (Habenstein and Lamers, 1962:414–415).

Death was a more common occurrence in some age categories in the past, as Table 1-1 indicates. In addition, death was not mainly the property of the elderly. Children died at a dramatically higher rate, as did youths and adults. It is only in the age group 45 to 54 that the rate for 1982 surpasses the rate for 1900. What this means is that in 1900 you probably couldn't pass through childhood without experiencing the deaths of several members of your family, old, young, and in-between.

During the first half of this century, however, death faded from public view. Death was less often defined in religious terms; it was increasingly seen in a secular framework. Life began and ended in this world; death was an end and not a passage to a sacred afterlife. As time passed, fewer people died at home and more died in hospitals. The handling of the dead was turned over to funeral directors. Crepe on doors and mourning dress began to disappear. Talking about death came to be regarded as impolite, and, when it was considered absolutely necessary, it was disguised by euphemisms.

In the second half of the twentieth century, death reemerged as a topic of public discourse. (Of course, death itself had never disappeared, only its public acknowledgment.) The study of death has also grown. Robert Fulton (1976:xiii) estimated that more material on

Table 1-1   Death Rates per One Thousand Population by Age, U.S. 1900[a] and 1982[b] and Ratio of Death Rates by Age to Overall Death Rates, U.S. 1900 and 1982.

AGE	1900	RATIO	1982	RATIO
All Ages	17.2	1.0	8.5	1.0
Under 1	162.4	9.44	11.6	1.36
1–4	19.8	1.15	0.6	.07
5–14	3.9	.23	0.3	.04
15–24	5.9	.34	1.0	.12
25–34	8.2	.48	1.3	.15
35–44	10.2	.59	4.2	.49
45–54	15.0	.87	11.0	1.29
55–64	27.2	1.58	26.2	3.08
65–74	56.4	3.28	29.5	3.47
75–84	123.3	7.17	66.7	7.85
85 and over	260.9	15.17	150.5	17.70

[a]Data from U.S. Bureau of the Census (1975:28).
[b]Data from National Center for Health Statistics (1984:10).

death appeared in scholarly journals between 1970 and 1975 than in the preceding one hundred years. Over one thousand courses on death are offered in American colleges and universities (Fulton, 1976:xiv). Television documentaries, films, newspaper articles, songs, and everyday conversations about death all signal the return of death to public view.

The obvious question is what factors explain this surge in the popularity of the topic of death.[1] There were several factors involved in the increased interest in death. It should be understood that these factors all emerged at about the same time and that it was their convergence that constituted the critical mass necessary for interest to grow.

A major factor is demographic, the reaching of death age of the same generation whose extended life expectancy had promoted the growth of gerontology, geriatrics, retirement communities, and public concern for the problems of the elderly. The greatest rise in life expectancy in one decade during this century occurred between 1940 and 1950, jumping 62.9 to 68.2. In other words, a population swell was now living past retirement and then dying in great numbers. This meant that a generation grew up without experiencing the death of a grandparent until adolescence (Fulton, 1965:79). Suddenly, unprepared by other deaths, a cohort of young people faced death in the family. In addition to the focus on the elderly themselves, interest in death was sparked by coverage of the experience of that cohort of young people whose every twitch was chronicled by the media.

A second factor in the growing interest in death was the developments in medicine and health care that enabled life to be prolonged and raised a series of moral questions regarding that prolongation of life and also of dying (Freeman, Brim, and Williams, 1970:xix–xx; Lofland, 1978:74). Now that dying patients could be kept alive technologically, the question was raised of whether a life tied to machines was worth sustaining.

One issue, in short, centered on the quality of life. Since the body could now be kept alive while the brain, and some would say the humanity, had "died," the issue of the definition of death was also raised. The American fascination with medical developments such as organ transplants and artificial hearts reflected in the extensive media coverage of the personnel, the procedures, and the recipients of those developments, contributed to keeping death and life-and-death struggles in public view.

The war in Vietnam made death an everyday staple of American lives. Media coverage of the war was greater than that of any war in history. Television news programs and newspapers featured regular "body counts" of dead soldiers from both sides. News footage showed the dead and dying on television newscasts several times a day. While it often had the unreality of anything depicted within the confines of a small screen in a small box in your living room, it was still exposure of a sort. It wasn't simply the casualties of the war that generated interest in death. It was also the protest against the war (Freeman, Brim, Williams, 1970:xx). That protest called into question the meaning of those deaths; that is, it made those sacrifices more poignant by suggesting that they might have been made in vain. Finally, the military dead in the war in Vietnam, as in all wars, were the young. They died at a time when young people in general were being invested with a kind of saintliness, and constituted the center of gravity of American popular culture (Kamerman, 1975). Only a war fought by children would have generated greater emotional power.

Another factor that stimulated interest in death was the threat of a nuclear holocaust and the parallel threat of environmental catastrophe. Edwin Shneidman (1973) saw nuclear megadeath as the backdrop of contemporary life, particularly for young people who "cannot be assured of a future" (181). He wrote, "One cannot fail to include this overhanging threat of violent mass death as one of the vitally important items in the total array of forces that, consciously or unconsciously, have shaped our current views of life and death" (180–181).

As important as the threat of megadeath may have been in sparking interest in death and as awesome and terrible as the menace itself remains, the current influence of this factor should not be overestimated. Vast spaces often lie between a threat and people's perceptions of the threat. Raymond L. Schmitt (1982–83) in fact argues that ordinary Americans don't get very worked up about the threat of nuclear holocaust because of "inhibiting mechanisms" (109) that neutralize its impact. One such factor is the irrelevance of nuclear weapons to everyday life. As Schmitt puts it:

> Nuclear weapons do not have much to do with Americans' everyday role-identities or idealized selves; they have little effect on being a good parent or obtaining recognition in one's field. (111)

Americans don't have much of the information about the grim side of nuclear research because this research is veiled in secrecy. Even when the dangers break through into public view, for example, the near catastrophe at the Three Mile Island nuclear power plant, Americans' general optimism and faith in science's ability to master nature restore calm (111). In addition, if it is difficult in general for people to contemplate their own deaths, "How much more difficult it is for those who have not lived through a Hiroshima-type experience to contemplate *collective* death" (112).

The chilling effect of these mechanisms is to make it difficult for most Americans to take seriously the threat of nuclear obliteration. Never in sight, never in mind!

The same, of course, is true of environmental disaster. Although its threat is often taken as another force generating interest in death (e.g., Charmaz, 1980:8–9), it must also be examined in light of Schmitt's findings. It is only to the extent that people experience environmental calamity in their own lives that they take the threat seriously. The fact that small environmental disasters occur on a fairly regular basis tends to remind us that the threat exists. However, widespread ecological catastrophe probably seems as distant as nuclear annihilation. It is certainly leavened by the same American optimism and faith in science that affects Americans' perceptions of nuclear war.

In sum, the vision of nuclear and ecological destruction may have had an effect in generating interest in death, but its influence was probably confined to specific segments of the population in a specific era and was not as important as some would prefer to believe.

A final factor in the growth of interest in death was the increase in the perceived tempo and certainly in the coverage of violence in the 1960s. Urban disturbances with accompanying loss of life spread to most major American cities. Violent death, as Geoffrey Gorer (1965:197) points out, in a society whose members, particularly the young, have little experience with death, has the fascination of "pornography." Urban crime and street violence, combined with coverage of the war in Vietnam, made the sight of death difficult to avoid. Although the image was sometimes distorted, the stimulus to interest was there nonetheless.

Interest in death began to grow because of the convergence of the forces just mentioned; it was stimulated and sustained by the publication of certain books. The publication of Elisabeth Kübler-Ross's (1969) *On Death and Dying* was a significant stimulus to the growth in popularity of the subject of death. The collections edited by Herman Feifel (1959), *The Meaning of Death*, and Robert Fulton (1965), *Death and Identity*, performed the same function in the social sciences. These books should be seen as both reflection and reinforcement of the interest that was growing in the area of death and dying.

Interest in death was also promoted by individuals and organizations whose efforts can be collectively referred to as "the death and dying movement" (Charmaz, 1980:10–12). Under this linguistic umbrella are, among others, people interested in improving the quality of dying in hospitals, people interested in promoting the spread of hospice care, people interested in protecting the rights of dying patients, people interested in the moral questions involved in the legal definition of death, and people interested in streamlining the funeral. Again, these movements are both promoters and products of the growing interest in death.

More recently, the growth of terrorist violence keeps death in front of people's eyes. As with the nuclear and ecological threats, the degree to which terrorist violence keeps mortality in view depends on how closely you are touched, or are likely to be touched by it. The specter of death by terrorism is, at any rate, raised almost daily in the media. It is to the continuance of attention to death what urban violence in the 1960s was to the growth of attention to death.

RECENT TRENDS IN DEATH AND DYING

Although in one sense death is a constant in human history (all people die), its frequency, distribution, and meaning vary widely from one time to another and from one place to another. Just as the public attention paid to death has changed in the last one hundred years, so has the character of death and dying.

There has been a shift in the meaning of death from a process interpreted in a sacred framework to one interpreted in a secular framework (Fulton, 1976:3–4). Death is less and less seen as part of a divine plan, one step in the course through life to the afterlife. Instead, death is seen as being merely a part of this world, the final part, and nothing more. In a sense it has lost its meaning.

Without a sacred meaning to neutralize its evil, death has become almost "dirty," not fit for polite society. The shift toward a secular conception of death has meant a confrontation with the finality of death. Americans, Herman Feifel (1959:xv) points out, have reacted by trying to avoid death and the dying and by trying to deny the existence of death. Much of the American response to death for most of this century is an example of one or both of these patterns.

One mechanism of avoidance is that the handling of the dead has been turned over to funeral directors. In the past, bodies were laid out for viewing in the home. While an undertaker might have been called in, the family often participated in the preparation of the body. The growth of the funeral industry during this century allowed people to avoid this increasingly unpleasant contact with the dead.

Another trend, in part a consequence of the shift in the meaning of death and in part a reflection of deritualization in American society in general, is the streamlining of mourning. Not only do people mourn for less time than a century ago, but the rituals and displays that characterized mourning in the last century have given way to more and more cursory and unadorned behaviors. These are the residue of the attacks on the funeral and the funeral industry that began in the 1960s. The formation of memorial societies, whose goal is to enable their members to arrange cheap and simple funerals, is a good indication of this trend.

Although most people follow some version (albeit scaled down) of the traditional funeral, their bereavement has fewer institutionalized supports. In addition, the course of bereavement has been influenced by the temporal norms of the business world (Pratt, 1981). People are given limited time off for mourning, and then only for certain losses. In this way, not only has mourning become deritualized, it has also become rationalized, in Weber's (1958a:51) meaning of the term. By quantifying mourning into units of time and money, it becomes more easily calculable and predictable.

Demographically, death has become more and more the property of the old. In 1900, children under 15 constituted about 34 percent of the U.S. population, but about 53 percent of the total number of deaths. People over 65 constituted about 4 percent of the U.S. population, but about 17 percent of the total number of deaths (Fulton, 1976:5).

In sharp contrast, in 1982 children under 15 constituted about 22 percent of the population, but only 3 percent of the total number of deaths. People over 65 made up about 12 percent of the population, but almost 69 percent of deaths (National Center for Health Statistics, 1984:10; U.S. Bureau of the Census, 1984:29). This demographic shift is reflected in our assumption that when a child dies something must have gone wrong; it needs to be explained. When an old person dies, the cause may be a question, but the death itself is hardly out of the ordinary. Because a stigma still attaches to death in America, the old are marked as the carriers of death.

The scene of death has shifted from the home to the institution. As late as 1949, less than half (49.5 percent) of the people who died in the United States died in institutions (Lerner, 1970:22). In 1982, the figure was over two-thirds (68.1%).[2] This shift has had several consequences. First, the dying and near-dying are isolated from the rest of society in hospitals, old age homes, and nursing homes. That avoidance of the dying makes the denial of death that much easier. In addition, children are not allowed in most hospitals, so their insulation from death is even more complete. Finally, dying in institutions embeds death in the bureaucratic structure of those institutions (Blauner, 1966). The dying must conform to the routines and schedules of hospital life and spend their final time in the care of often impersonal, sometimes cold, strangers.

These changes perhaps symbolize the growing irrelevance of the dying in American society. As Blauner (1966) points out, in simple village societies the death of any individual is potentially disruptive to village life. This disruption is reflected in the intensity, extent, and communal quality of mourning. In modern mass societies, the death of any one individual, with the possible exception of societal leaders, fails to move many of us because no one death has the power to disrupt a community's life. The disturbance caused by an individual's death is felt, if at all, only by the immediate family, and consequently it is left to the immediate family to handle mourning. As our life is of little consequence to our community, so too is our death.

This irrelevance is exacerbated by the prolongation of dying and the concentration of dying in an age group whose lives are also largely irrelevant to the smooth functioning of modern societies, the elderly. As Fulton and Fulton (1971) point out, the death of an elderly family member may be preceded by a separation from the family caused by confinement in a hospital, old age home, or nursing home. The same is also true of self-imposed isolation in retirement communities. This is not to say that this is the purpose of such removal, although it certainly is in some cases, but rather that it is a latent function, that is, an unintended consequence of the shift of dying to institutions and the growth of colonies of old people. Grief begins, the Fultons maintain, at the point of initial separation from the family. By the time old people die, they are irrelevant to the family system and their deaths are anticlimactic. The irrelevance of the death of any one individual to the functioning of society has its counterpart in the irrelevance of the death of the family members most likely to die, old people, to the functioning of the family. Grief may be generated, but is not always overpowering. Although this may change as the population ages and the elderly become a more substantial market, the Fultons' characterization of the place of the elderly remains overwhelmingly accurate today.

THE APPROACH OF THIS BOOK

Death in America can be studied for its own sake, as a mirror to understand American society in general, and as an opportunity to elucidate sociological concepts. The purpose of this book is to do all three.

The first two parts of the book lay a groundwork of concepts and empirical work in the sociological study of death and dying. The basic areas in the study of death—death, dying, grief, bereavement, and mourning—are covered in these first two sections. This material is applied in the third part to specific topics selected for their inherent interest as well as for their usefulness as illustrations of the points made earlier.

To say that death and dying are emotion-laden topics understates the case. In a sense, they are *the* emotion-laden topics. In social science in general, it is necessary to try to suspend the value judgments that dominate conversations and analyses in everyday life. In the study of death, since the temptation to sermonize is much greater, this control is doubly necessary. The postscript is a concession to the emotional power of death. In it, the major arguments of the book are restated and an excerpt from a paper by psychologists John P. Brantner is reprinted. Brantner's paper, entitled "Death and the Self," is formally a discussion of the utility of death education in our confrontation with death. It is also a personal and moving celebration of life lived forever in the face of death.

SUMMARY

The theme of this book is the interface of American life and American death. Although death is a constant in history, its meaning, frequency, and distribution change over time and between places.

Death was more openly discussed in America until the early part of this century. Death as a topic for public discussion and a phenomenon for public view almost disappeared until the late 1950s. At about that time, the public attention to death began growing, until now it has become almost popular.

The reasons for the rise in attention to death were discussed. These include the dying off of the generation of old people whose life expectancy had been dramatically extended between 1940 and 1950, developments in medicine that prolonged life and dying and raised both moral issues and questions about the definition of death, the war in Vietnam and the protest against it, and the threat of nuclear and ecological catastrophe. Once interest developed, the publication of popular books on death and the formation of movements around death-related issues promoted continuing interest. The threat of death from terrorist violence also played a role.

Recent trends in death and dying were examined. There has been a shift from a sacred to a secular view of death. Because of this, Americans tended to react to the finality of death by avoiding it and denying it. Funerals have become more streamlined and rationalized. In addition, death has become the property of the old. The scene of death has shifted from the home to the institution. This has isolated the dying, cut children off from exposure to death and dying, and brought dying under bureaucratic control. In part, this isolation reflects the decreasing power in mass society of single deaths to disrupt the functioning of the community. The elderly, as Robert Fulton suggests, are isolated, stigmatized, because death is stigmatized, and emotionally cut off through anticipatory grieving.

The design of the book was delineated. After covering the basic areas in the study of death, that is, death, dying, grief, bereavement, and mourning, in the first two sections, that analysis is developed in the third section by applying it to more specialized topics.

A postscript has been added to acknowledge the emotional power of death and to articulate what should be obvious: that sociology is not only *about* people, but also *by* people.

Notes

1. This analysis of the rise in attention to death in the past twenty-five years is an amalgam of the work of Robert Fulton (1976; 1981); Howard E. Freeman, Orville G. Brim, Jr., and Greer Williams (1970); Edwin Shneidman (1973; 1984); and Kathy Charmaz (1980), with additions and refinements of my own.

2. Personal communication from the Division of Vital Statistics, National Center for Health Statistics, Hyattsville, Md., August 13, 1985.

CHAPTER TWO

THE SOCIAL CONSTRUCTION OF DYING AND DEATH

The notion of *social construction*, that our conceptions of reality are more a function of the way we look at the world than of the world itself, is one of the most basic in sociology. We tend to see the world as being "out there" to be discovered, and so we tend to neglect our own prior part in formulating that world.[1]

This idea of the plasticity of the world was very neatly expressed by W. I. Thomas (Thomas and Thomas, 1928:572) in the concept, *definition of the situation*: "If men define situations as real, they are real in their consequences." We define situations in a certain way and then act as though they were that way all along. Put another way, we don't react to raw stimuli, as we assume rats and pigeons do, but to our interpretation of those stimuli, that is, to the *meanings* they have for us (Stone and Farberman, 1970:15).

The study of any area of human behavior is really a study of how meanings in that area are established, sustained, threatened, changed, lost, and restored. Those meanings are all to a degree personal constructions, but the building blocks and rules of construction are provided by society. The process of social construction takes place on two inextricably connected levels: in relation to dying, (1) in the general norms and values relating to proper behavior including proper dying and (2) in the behavior of the dying and of people around them, including interaction between them; and in relation to death, (1) in the formulation of definitions like the legal definitions of death and (2) in the practical actions of people like physicians in applying interpretations of that definition in "producing" death determinations.

We take these constructions for granted until there is trouble. When our assumptions are challenged, for example, by the rise of rival definitions, our cultural and temporal biases are exposed.[2]

The remainder of this chapter is an analysis of the social construction of death and the social construction of dying out of which death often comes.

THE SOCIAL CONSTRUCTION OF DYING

Death comes out of dying. This seems so obvious that it doesn't warrant mention, but sometimes, as in sudden death, it doesn't happen that way. It is only when problems occur in that "natural" sequence that the socially constructed character of death and dying is exposed.

For example, David Sudnow (1967a:95–96) describes a patient who was being operated on for a gunshot wound. The patient died on the operating table although the wound hadn't seemed serious. Because the family hadn't been prepared for the patient's death, the staff created a dying story that would make sense of the outcome of death.

They came out several times to the patient's family, each time intimating a worsening of the patient's condition. "After several progressively more solemn prognostications, the occurrence of death was announced, now placed within a history of 'dying' " (96). Sudnow also mentions that almost every announcement of death includes a remark on past history designed to make the death seem the endpoint of an orderly sequence. For example, "Mrs. Jones, apparently Mr. Jones had a heart attack this afternoon and his body was too weak to fight it and he passed away" (133).

Dying as a Role Career

People play many roles. These roles are played over time. A person's history in a role is called a *role career*. Careers have objective and subjective elements (Hughes, 1937), that is, a sequence of events or a chronology, and a sequence of changes in self-image. These changes in self-image are judged by values attached to particular roles in particular societies or organizational settings. Compare, for example, the standards for being a good worker in a contemporary American office and in a nineteenth-century English mill.

The phases of a career sometimes follow orderly sequences. These phases are then described as stages. One popular stage model is Elisabeth Kübler-Ross's stages of dying (which will be analyzed in Chapter Four). Here it will only be pointed out that hospital staff, armed with this model, tend to interpret the events of a patient's dying as fitting into one or another of these stages. So that, having imposed some structure on the world, that structured world is now seen as prior evidence of the justice of that imposition.

An important feature of all careers is that they have a *retroactive character*. The events of the past are reinterpreted to make sense of the present (Mead, 1932; 1938) as the death and subsequent "dying" of the gunshot victim described by Sudnow clearly illustrates. In the same way, although more self-consciously, the "facts" of a life are reconstructed in case histories to make sense of some outcome, for example, hospitalization in a mental institution. In that case, a patient's past is reinterpreted to demonstrate "that all along he had been becoming sick, that he finally became very sick, and that if he had not been hospitalized much worse things would have happened to him" (Goffman, 1961:145). As will be discussed in Chapter Eight, coroners reconstruct the lives of the subjects of their investigations to make sense of a suicidal or nonsuicidal conclusion, much as juries do with guilty or innocent outcomes.

From a sociological point of view, what dying means is a function of the overall values of our society (see Chapter Three) and the norms and values inherent in the settings in which we die (see Chapter Four), all, of course, processed by our idiosyncratic selves. We use these values as models to decide whether or not we are dying well or poorly.

Awareness Contexts and Dying-Role Careers[3]

Definitions of the situation influence the course of interaction. In the case of patients dying in a hospital, a definition crucial to the interaction between patients and staff is whether or not patients know they are dying. Glaser and Strauss (1965) described four such *awareness contexts.*

In *closed awareness,* the staff knows that the patient is dying, but the patient does not. Closed awareness influences the interaction between patients and both staff and family. Family may find it difficult to sustain the lie or, on the other hand, may prefer the equanimity a semblance of normality allows. Nurses, who spend blocks of time with a patient (as opposed to physicians who may visit a patient for a few minutes each day), may face closed awareness with the same options as family, though, of course, in a lower emotional key.

In *suspicion awareness,* the patient suspects that he or she is dying and the staff is aware of the patient's suspicions. Patients often engage in frantic efforts to discover the truth. Again, both the family and the staff, particularly the nurse, feel the strain of resisting a patient's attempts to gain information.

In *mutual pretense,* both the patient and staff know that the patient is dying, but act as though that weren't the case. If the patient initiates the pretense, it allows the dignity of choosing and having that choice honored. For the family, mutual pretense leaves many things unsaid. Mutual pretense is sustained by an elaborate etiquette, for example, avoiding "dangerous" topics or only discussing them if no one breaks down. If the pretense is threatened, everyone must act as though nothing has happened. "Thus, a nurse may take special pains to announce herself before entering a patient's room so as not to surprise him at his crying" (Glaser and Strauss, 1965:73).

In *open awareness,* staff and patient openly acknowledge the patient's impending death. Open awareness raises the issues of the time of death and the style of dying. While it allows the possibility of ending life as the patient would wish, it also opens up the opposite possibility, that is, that the patient may die, in John Brantner's (1971:18) words, "with projects unfinished, with things undone, and with secrets poorly concealed." The interaction between patient and staff may become a negotiation focusing on compliance with certain routines, for example, taking medication or eating, or on the determination of the amount of time and conversation that passes between nurse and patient (94–95). If open awareness makes a patient's dying easier, it also makes it easier for family and staff. The opposite is also true.

Several career paths are possible, constituted by combinations of these awareness contexts (see Figure 2.1). There is nothing inevitable about the movement from one awareness context to another. In addition, some patients begin and end their dying careers in only one of the four contexts.

Movement through a role career is dependent on *career contingencies* (Hughes, 1965:455–458; Goffman, 1961:134–136). These often large-scale factors make one or another dying-role career and awareness context more likely. Contingencies promoting a closed awareness include a model of the professional–patient relationship that makes the professional a high priest with charismatic powers (Wilson, 1970:20–21) and the patient a lowly supplicant. As the character of that relationship becomes more egalitarian (Zola and Miller, 1973), closed awareness becomes a less likely alternative. As part of the same trend, the increase in malpractice suits and the patients' rights movement make closed awareness even less likely. Physicians now fear the legal ramifications of withholding information. This in turn is one consequence of the struggle between the medical and legal professions for territory.

Because the character of the relationship has not completely shifted, suspicion awareness remains a likely possibility. Patients almost categorically expect to be lied to or at least not told the complete truth. This is less a function of a suspicious personality than of the nature of the patient role.

Another contingency influencing the probability of one career path being followed rather than another is the openness with which death is discussed in the society at large. This certainly influences the willingness of physicians to discuss death with their patients. Glaser and Strauss's (1965:30–31) observation that American physicians tend not to tell patients of impending death because death, as it is with many Americans, is a taboo subject was certainly truer in 1965 than it

FIGURE 2-1 CAREER PATHS THROUGH AWARENESS CONTEXTS

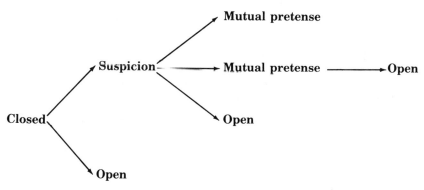

is today. It makes sense that as death becomes less taboo a subject for many Americans, it will become less taboo a subject for American physicians as well.

Finally, it should be noted that, to an extent, awareness contexts may vary with particular others. A patient may maintain open awareness with a physician, but mutual pretense with the family. Even within a family, a patient may maintain open awareness with a wife, be closed with a son, and engage in mutual pretense with a parent.

THE SOCIAL CONSTRUCTION OF DEATH

Just as the process of dying is socially constructed, so is its outcome, death. We usually take the definition of death for granted. But recent medical developments that allow life to be sustained past what would before have been death raise the question of when precisely someone has died. The question is the same as the question of when precisely life has begun, the crux of the controversy over abortion. Rather than being a self-evident reflection of the way the world "really" is, the moment of death, like the moment of life, is a question susceptible to many answers. These answers are social constructions, some informal, some, as in legal definitions of death, enacted.

Building Blocks in the Construction of Definitions of Death

Three interlocking social elements structure definitions of death: cultural, legal, and organizational/occupational.

The shift in Western societies from a sacred to a secular view of death (discussed in greater detail in Chapter Three), for example, created, in Orrin Klapp's (1969:vii) phrase, a "shortcoming of meaning." No longer able to define death as a natural stage in a divine process, it became of this world, "the consequence of personal neglect or untoward accident" (Fulton, 1965:4). It became something to be avoided and denied. In the previous chapter, the shift to more openness about death was analyzed. One ironic accompaniment to this openness is a continuing tendency to romanticize death. "Many of our current attitudes toward death," writes Edwin Shneidman (1973:66), in a chapter titled "On the Deromanticization of Death," "are unconsciously sentimental. The notions of 'heroic death,' of 'generatively,' of 'wise death' in mature old age are culture-laden rationalizations. It is pleasant to think that one can face the prospect of his own annihilation with true equanimity." Shneidman sees this romanticization as related to suicide. "Individuals who are suicidal suffer, among their other burdens, from a temporary loss of the view of death as the enemy" (66). He also points out America's "romanticization of killing in peacetime and of being killed in wartime" (66). It allows us to dehumanize others and, consequently, rob their deaths of tragedy. This, Shneidman claims, gives a surrealistic acceptability to death in issues like race relations and nuclear holocaust.

Changes and variations between states in legal definitions of death are another element in the social construction of death. Edwin H. Albano (1969:20) described the traditional bases of defining a person as dead:

> . . . when the heart stops beating and the person ceases to breathe and when at the same time the pupils remain fixed and dilated and there is an absence of tendon reflexes, the physician is legally justified in signing the death certificate.

More recent definitions of death have addressed the state of brain functioning on the grounds that personhood inheres in consciousness. When a person no longer has the potential for consciousness, he or she is a patchwork of tissues, organs, and cells, not a person. The issue was raised by the ability of medical science to keep a body alive with technology after the possibility for consciousness has disappeared. In response, states are enacting new legal definitions that take this issue into account. The California statute on the definition of death reads in part,

> A person shall be pronounced dead if it is determined by a physician that the person has suffered a total and irreversible cessation of brain function. (cited in Dornette, 1982:121)

A recent case illustrates the complexity of definitions of death and their application. In 1975, the parents of comatose Karen Ann Quinlan made the decision to remove the respirator they thought might be keeping her alive. Although she wasn't clearly *brain dead,* didn't clearly have permanent loss of all brain functions, she was in a persistent *vegetative state,* with a permanent loss of cognitive brain functions (Jonsen, Siegler, and Winslade, 1982:37–39). Removing her from the respirator was predicated on the feeling that she was being kept alive by extraordinary technological means and that if they were discontinued, she might die a "natural" death. But, in fact, she lived for about ten more years, in the same vegetative state, dying finally of pulmonary failure in 1985.

The question of precisely when a person is dead has become particularly important in the era of organ transplants. The sooner organs can be removed, the more useful they are for transplantation. This not only rests on when a person is dead, but on who has the legitimate right to make that pronouncement. All states currently require a physician to make that determination. Some states, however, are considering legislation that would allow others, such as nurses, to pronounce death. That would speed up the process considerably in some cases.

Some people fear that the need for fresh organs may encourage physicians in hospitals where transplants are done to pronounce death earlier than they would if there were no such pressure. Obviously, the definition of death is also influenced by organizational and occupational considerations. In studying the social organization of death work in two hospitals from the point of view of staff, David Sudnow (1967a) defined death and dying operationally as the procedures that are invoked when those words are spoken. This is an interesting position or *study policy* to adopt.[4] It allows us to see the extent to which ordinarily emotion-laden events like death and dying can become humdrum work matters [in Everett Hughes's (1958:54–55) words, the extent to which your emergency becomes their routine]. This is certainly a feature of all jobs that involve, over and over again, other people's emergencies. With perceptivity, Sudnow points out that a career stage at work is passed when nurses, for example, after mentioning their first patient's death, their second, and so on, have experienced so many that they lose count.

But the other meanings of death and dying to hospital staff are also important. Not all deaths are equally matters of procedure. Some deaths touch staff personally, particularly those of patients with whom staff identify (Hale, Schmitt, and Leonard, 1984). The social value of the person is also relevant in itself and because, presumably, staff identify with patients in part based on presumed shared values and common value.

In addition to occupational considerations, organizational contexts influence the meanings of death. Sudnow (1970:202–204) mentions a tendency of house staff and interns in one hospital he studied to concentrate on interesting cases, giving the others less, though not necessarily improper, care. Another factor influencing care was the number of other patients a physician was responsible for. These two organizational realities, psychological value in a teaching hospital and constraints placed on staff by the size of the patient population, affected the efforts expended by staff in warding off death.

The social value of patients (detailed in Chapter Three) also affects the definition of their deaths. Sudnow (1967a:101) mentions two cases brought into the emergency room on the same day, both exhibiting signs of death: no pulse, no heartbeat, no breathing. Heroic efforts were made to resuscitate the first, a child, who was in fact revived for several hours. No such efforts were made to revive the second patient, an elderly woman. In effect, social value made one patient almost dead and the other already dead.

In summary, these definitions, cultural, legal, and organizational/occupational, act as career contingencies moving a person from dying to dead.

A SPECIAL CASE OF DYING TO DEAD: SOCIAL DEATH

David Sudnow (1967a) in *Passing On,* probably the major sociological work on the social construction of death, distinguishes three meanings of death:

> A tentative distinction can be made between "clinical death": the appearance of "death signs" upon physical examination; "biological death": the cessation of cellular activity; and a third category, "social death" which, within the hospital setting, is marked by that point at which a patient is treated as a corpse, though perhaps still "clinically" and "biologically" alive. (74)

Social death is the outcome of one dying-role career. Sudnow doesn't use social death in a general way, to mean being ignored or being socially isolated.[5] It is only when that definition leads to behavior appropriate to people clinically dead that the concept applies. For example, permissions for autopsies were signed, treatments were suspended, and/or "bodies" were partially wrapped. In at least some of these cases, he claims, suspension of treatment might have had the result of hastening clinical death, in effect, acting as a self-fulfilling prophecy.

The social value of the patient was a major career contingency in moving someone toward social death: old before young, poor before rich. Consequently, a person's social attributes determined quite literally their life chances.

SUMMARY

Our notions of reality, including our conceptions of death, are socially constructed. We tend to take these notions for granted until we are jarred into realizing our part in creating them. The rise of competing versions of reality, for example, new legal definitions of death, is one basis for this realization. But these definitions are in fact tied to particular places in particular times.

Not only are conceptions of death social constructions, but so are the meanings of dying. If someone dies over a sufficient time, dying can become a role career. People are socialized into that role, judge themselves by the standards attached to that role, and move through their careers because of the operation of career contingencies. Dying careers, as all role careers, have a retroactive character and are also influenced by the settings in which dying takes place.

One example of how definitions of dying influence interaction is the concept of awareness context. The four awareness contexts described by Glaser and Strauss entail four probable interactional scripts. These awareness contexts are in turn made more or less likely by large-scale factors like cultural values and changes in the professional–patient relationship.

Definitions of death are constructed on several levels: cultural, legal, and organizational/occupational. They are worked out, for example, in the everyday worlds of hospital staff doing death work.

A particularly clear example of this process of definition is the category called social death. People may be treated as clinically dead before in fact they are. And this treatment is clearly tied to social attributes and values. There is nothing inevitable or self-evident about defining someone as being socially dead; it is a judgment made by specific people, for particular reasons, in given circumstances.

There should be nothing really surprising about this social construction. If we create the meanings of life, we also create the meanings of death.

Notes

1. See Blumer (1969) and Berger and Luckmann (1966) for extended analyses of this idea.

2. This is the crux of ethnocentrism and temporocentrism.

3. In this chapter, awareness contexts are discussed as they relate to dying-role careers. In Chapter Four, the discussion focuses on those aspects of hospital structure that support various awareness contexts.

4. This is something of an injustice to the ethnomethodological position Sudnow adopts. His emphasis is on how death and dying are produced as meaningful occurrences. For present purposes, however, the other meanings of death and dying from the staff point of view, for example, a professional failure, a personal tragedy, are also important. They speak to the question of whether or not that is all death is from the point of view of staff.

5. It would be interesting, though, to study social death when the term "death" is used in a metaphorical rather than a literal sense. The definition of

a political outcast as a "nonperson" is one example of this fascinating, poignant role career. The late Russian composer Dmitri Shostakovich (1979) described how an unfavorable mention in *Pravda* sent the friends of the hapless musician hurrying to their music rooms to destroy all traces of association with him. Pictures were ripped up, music was thrown out, phonograph records were smashed, and so forth. Such an occurrence was often followed by the permanent disappearance of the unfortunate musician. This is very similar to Sudnow's (1967a:77) description of the husband who almost died in the hospital, survived, came home to find his wife had removed his clothes and begun to make funeral arrangements, had a heart attack, and died.

CHAPTER THREE
DEATH AND SOCIAL VALUES

Our attitudes toward death and dying are embedded in our social values. Our values affect the way we conceptualize death. Do we see it as a tragedy or as a release from earthly woes? Do we see it, as Fulton (1976:3–5) suggests, as a personal failure? Is it any longer a moral matter or has it become a technological one (Cassell, 1975:43–48)?

Values also affect our behavior in relation to death because values underlie the guidelines on which we base our behavior. Do we avoid contact with death and the things and people associated with death? Do we shudder when a person we're introduced to mentions, as he extends his hand toward us, that he's a funeral director?

More specifically, values affect the way we treat the dying. Do we change our behavior when a sick friend's illness is diagnosed as fatal, as studies indicate health care personnel do toward dying patients? Do we gather around the dying as the families of Chinese patients in Malaysian hospitals do, so that our relatives literally die in the midst of their loved ones (Glaser and Strauss, 1965:81)? Or do we instead segregate out the dying in hospitals, which isolates them and insulates children and often adults from the process of dying and from death itself?

This chapter considers some major American values and how they affect attitudes and behavior related to death and dying. This is not to suggest that values by themselves completely explain attitudes toward death and dying. Changes in social structure and other factors of course play an important part. On the other hand, it is a mistake to minimize the influence that values have on behavior.

Although many values affect our behavior, the focus will be on the following values that have an especially important effect on our attitudes and behavior toward death: (1) the shift from a *sacred to a secular* orientation toward life and death, (2) the *Protestant ethos* and the values subsumed by it, (3) *science and the mastery of nature,* and (4) *future orientation.*

THE SHIFT FROM A SACRED TO A SECULAR VIEW OF DEATH

One of the major trends in the Western world over the past few centuries has been the gradual secularization of more and more areas of life. This involved the removal of areas from the realm of religious interpretation and control. As life was increasingly dominated by secularization, so also was death.

Robert Fulton and Gilbert Geis (1962) maintain that when death was defined in a religious framework, it seemed a natural event, part of God's plan. There was conception, birth, life, death, and afterlife. As the Western world moved farther away from the traditional Judeo–Christian conception of Heaven, death became an event of this world, the absolutely final event.

After abandoning their belief in an afterlife, people were left alone with the finality of their own death. Faced with their mortality, people chose avoidance and denial to neutralize the awesome intransigence of death (Feifel, 1959:xv; 1977:4–5). As David Stannard wrote (1977:194), "In a world bereft of ultimate meaning either in life or in death—in which neither the community of the living nor the vision of a mystical but literal afterlife any longer provides solace—modern man, in the face of fate, has been forced to choose between the alternatives of outright avoidance or a secularized masquerade."

Avoidance is simply the attempt to steer clear of death and dying. Treating death as a taboo subject, for example, is the avoidance of death in conversation. Avoiding death makes denial easier.

Denial is, in a sense, looking at death but mistaking it for something less final. In euphemisms, we deny death its full power by claiming, for example, that it isn't really death, but rather going on a trip. "Elvis [Presley] didn't die," in the words of a bumper sticker marketed shortly after his death. "He just moved on to a better town."

In contrast to this analysis, some social scientists have argued that America is not a death-denying society at all, but rather a death-accepting society. Parsons and Lidz (1967:133–170) claim that since the denial of death is inconsistent with the American commitment to scientific values as well as the dominant pattern of activism (135), the orientation to death in American society has to be acceptance. In addition, they argue that some of the behavior usually mentioned as evidence of denial is really evidence of acceptance. Funeral directors disguising the body with cosmetics, which many claim is an evidence of denial, Parsons and Lidz claim is precisely the opposite. It comes, they say, from the "strong tendency in our individualistic, activistic society to want the deceased to appear in a manner that makes his former active capacities recognizable" (155). Consequently, it facilitates saying goodbye to the deceased.

While the acceptance–denial controversy will be better understood after more evidence is presented later in this chapter, it seems safe to say here that what disguising the body may facilitate is more a "bon voyage" for the great trip than a confrontation with the finality of death. As Philippe Ariès (1975:22–23) wrote, "In modern America chemical techniques for preserving the body make us forget death by creating an illusion of life . . . this is the first time that a whole society has honored the dead by pretending they were alive."

Perhaps the most tenable position begins by recognizing that denial and acceptance coexist in the American character (Dumont and Foss, 1972:95). It is then possible to point out that American society is moving slowly in the direction of acceptance, although the overall picture still remains one of denial and avoidance (Charmaz, 1980:12). Or, put another way, to say that things are changing is not to say that things have changed.

With that said, I will examine the avoidance, denial, acceptance argument in greater detail.

Avoidance and Denial

In contemporary American society, death and the dying are avoided at many stages and in many ways. To begin at the end, the corpse itself is avoided by turning over its handling to funeral directors. Until well into the nineteenth century, the family participated with the undertaker in laying out the dead. This was most often done at home. Now the dead are brought to funeral "homes."

Because more than half of all people who die in the United States each year die in institutions (hospitals, old age homes, etc.), the dying can be avoided. They die out of our sight. In addition, hospitals have rules that keep children out, minimizing their chance to view the process of dying. Because family and friends cannot live at the hospital, they cannot live through a patient's dying.

In sum, dying is no longer an ordinary part of our lives occurring in ordinary places. Death is removed to special areas. When it does occur "off limits," for example, on the street or at home, it becomes that much more shocking.

Not only are the dead and the dying avoided, but those most likely to die, the carriers of death, the elderly, often withdraw from our view to old age homes, retirement communities, and the like. "The aged, those most susceptible to death, seek in ever-increasing numbers to remove themselves to segregated retirement communities to await fate in the same manner as the leper once did" (Fulton 1967:4).

Death is also avoided in conversation. It is still to a great extent a taboo subject. Although perhaps less so than before, as a topic of conversation death is still clearly out of the ordinary. Geoffrey Gorer (1965:192–199) has even suggested that death has become as dirty a subject in the present era as sex was in the Victorian era. Because of this, a pornography of death has arisen. This pornography, for example, violence in horror movies, is the French postcard of our day and will thrive as long as death remains "unmentionable in polite society" (Gorer, 1965:199).

In sum, death has been banished, both metaphorically and literally, from the normal arenas of our lives.

The second response to the shift from a secular orientation toward death is denial. The funeral director's attempt to make the corpse seem more lifelike is one example of the denial of death. People visiting a funeral home sometimes comment on how healthy and radiant the "loved one" appears.

Euphemisms are a second example of the denial of death. The purpose of a euphemism is to call something objectionable by a less offensive name in order to allow you to see a thing for what it's not. Going on a trip, for example, is generally more palatable than is dying. W. C. Fields's own epitaph was, after all, "On the whole, I'd rather be in Philadelphia." If you see buying a plot in a cemetery as a real estate investment, you can mobilize the feelings appropriate to real estate speculation, including the feeling that you'll be around to reap the profits.

The power of rhetoric and euphemisms is dramatically illustrated in the businesslike flatness of a series of letters that passed between the I. G. Farben Chemical Trust and the World War II concentration camp at Auschwitz (*Time*, 1947:33) As you read them, you have to keep reminding yourself that the lives of people, not the disposition of tractor parts, are being discussed:

> In contemplation experiments with a new soporific drug, we would appreciate your procuring for us a number of women.

> We received your answer but consider the price of 200 marks a woman excessive. We propose to pay not more than 170 marks a head. If agreeable, we will take possession of the women. We need approximately 150.

> We acknowledge your accord. Prepare for us 150 women in the best possible health conditions, and as soon as you advise us you are ready, we will take charge of them.

> Received the order of 150 women. Despite their emaciated condition, they were found satisfactory. We shall keep you posted on developments concerning this experiment.

> The tests were made. All subjects died. We shall contact you shortly on the subject of a new load.

A final example of denial is what Geoffrey Gorer (1965:85–87) calls "mummification." This involves the preservation by the bereaved of a room or house exactly as it was when the person died, "as though it were a shrine which would at any moment be reanimated" (85).

Why do we deny death? Dumont and Foss (1972:44–47) suggest that the socialization experiences of American children make it particularly difficult to handle death. American children have little firsthand experience with death, and when they do, the experience is often explained away, as in the case of the death of pets, with notions like "doggie heaven." Also, children's play often treats death as reversible.

In addition, television reduces the impact of death by turning even the real deaths shown into encapsulated media events that can be controlled in the same way all television can be controlled, that is, by turning the volume down or switching to another channel. Perhaps most important, the patterns of avoidance and denial that still characterize American culture in general became themes in the socialization of American children. As the adult society shifts toward a more accepting attitude toward death, so presumably will the attitudes of children shift in tandem.

The reasons why American children disregard death eventually become the basis for the adult denial of death. In addition, American culture defines death as the failure and life as the goal, and when life is so valuable, death becomes unthinkable.

On a societal level, denial is underwritten by the demographic trend that makes death seem the exclusive property of the elderly; that is, for the rest of us death is far in the future. In addition, the practices of avoidance, for example, keeping the dying out of our sight, make denial easier. Finally, the other values discussed in the paragraphs that follow contribute to our difficulty in handling the finality of death. To believe in the seemingly limitless control of nature afforded by science makes dealing with death's ultimate resistance to control hard to take.[1]

Although I'm sure almost everyone will recognize these patterns of avoidance and denial, it is certainly true that a shift has been taking place, if not necessarily toward acceptance of death, then certainly away from the avoidance and denial of death.[2]

As discussed in Chapter One, a number of factors converged in the 1950s and 1960s to produce a rise in public attention to death and dying. One concomitant of this trend was the growth in America of a movement of people whose goals were to change beliefs, emotional reactions, and behavior related to death and dying. Lyn Lofland (1978) calls them "the happy death movement." The movement is comprised of individuals and organizations who recommend three approaches to death and dying: *"Talk about it, rearrange it, and legislate it"* (78). Talking about death should be done in groups and classes. The goals of this death education range from helping people cope with fears about their own deaths to helping them deal with suicidal people (Eddy and Alles, 1983:11–12; Leviton, 1977:258–259). Rearranging death and dying would involve a shift of the scene of death from the institution to the home and the promotion of the hospice as an institutional setting for death. (The hospice movement, which seeks to humanize institutional death, is probably the clearest example of a move toward death acceptance.)

Legislating focuses on giving people control over their own dying through control over the manner and duration of medical treatment.

The happy death movement clearly represents concern with bringing death out into the open; that is, it is a confrontation of a sort. It is less clear that it represents as great or consistent an acceptance of death.

The growth of memorial societies is often seen as evidence of a more rational acceptance of death. These are organizations devoted to providing "no frills" funerals rather than the costly, to them wasteful, funeral arrangements often found in America. There are over 170 such societies in the United States and Canada, having a total of about three quarters of a million members (Consumers Union, 1977:212). Again, however, the display of a "rational " view of funeral expenditures does not necessarily reflect a change in basic attitudes toward death. In Robert Fulton's 1962 study (1971) of the attitudes toward death, grief, and funerals of nonmembers and members of memorial societies, the sample of memorial society members evidenced considerable ambivalence toward death. On the one hand, they expressed a pragmatic, nonmystical attitude toward death. On the other,

> This same group was most anxious of the three groups to avoid or disguise [death's] presence or possibility. This is demonstrated by such findings as their desire to eliminate the body from the funeral, their greater avoidance of funerals and their greater reluctance to permit their children to attend a funeral ceremony. (21)

The burgeoning of death courses in colleges and medical schools is also taken as evidence of the move toward greater acceptance. But again, the simple existence of these courses cannot be taken in itself as evidence of the acceptance of death. As Daniel Leviton (1977:257) wrote,

> When I first began teaching, my naive assumption was that death education would resolve existing fears or anxieties concerning death, and predispositions toward suicide. All participants would look forward to accomplishing the "healthiest" death, that is, *acceptance* of death. Initial research investigations indicated that the course did indeed reduce fear of death in some of the students. Others, however, evidence an increase in fear of death. Still others showed no change.

To summarize the denial–acceptance argument, although there

is clear evidence that death and dying are being discussed more openly, and that we are moving slowly away from denial and avoidance, it is hardly the same thing as saying that America is moving toward the acceptance of death. Whether acceptance will follow remains to be seen.

THE PROTESTANT ETHOS

The Protestant Ethos, particularly in its Puritan version, has always been a major theme in American culture. Although its formal theology has declined in importance since the Puritans landed in 1630, its influence is felt in many corners of American life from foreign policy to recreation (Lewis and Brissett, 1967) and from attitudes toward work to attitudes toward death.

To the Puritans, the world was rife with sin, and temptation was everywhere. Human institutions, such as the city or civilization in general, were corrupt. Only God's unspoiled creations, for example, nature, were pure. Since people were corrupt, they were not to be trusted (Weber, 1958b:106). Consequently, each individual was alone in the world, but for God.

The Puritans adopted the Calvinist doctrine of predestination. You were either one of the elect, predestined to go to Heaven, or one of the damned, predestined to go to Hell. Your fate was unalterable and unknowable, with certainty at least. What you could do, however, was evidence that you were one of the elect. "If one could do nothing to improve one's chance in the next world, one could at least convince others and oneself that the chances were good" (Anthony, 1977:42). The Puritans did this by avoiding temptation, by being pious, and by participating in the punishment of sinners and the destruction of evil. The Puritans didn't, by the way, try to "social work" the Devil; the Devil had to be destroyed. A less dramatic but especially important way of evidencing election was by working hard. The Protestant Ethic became in effect an ideology of work (Weber, 1958b: Anthony, 1977:40).

To the Puritans, death was an evil in the sense that it was brought into the world by original sin. On the other hand, death promised the reward of an afterlife for the chosen. Yet, by the doctrine of assurance, a person could never be sure of salvation. In fact, "Doubt of salvation was essential *to* salvation" (Stannard, 1977:83). Adding to this brew was the Puritan belief in the traditional Christian Hell, even though, at this time, this horrific image was losing favor in England (84). So, as Stannard wrote, "They did not fear death merely 'as children fear to go in the dark'; they feared it because they knew precisely what to expect from it" (89).

Stannard claims that during the eighteenth century there was a retrenchment. The doctrine of assurance waned, election could be viewed as less of an uncertainty, and death, though still to be feared, had lost some of its terror.

Their legacy, Puritan values strained through the contemporary experience, leaves us with a work ethic that has seeped into all areas of our lives, an individualism bordering on isolation, and a horror of death without the balancing comfort of a belief in eternal reward.

Kathy Charmaz (1980:12–15) claims that American attitudes toward death and dying are grounded in the Protestant Ethos. She describes this heritage as constituted by privation, independence, hard work, and individual achievement.

Death is a private matter. In Robert Fulton's words (1976:4), "Like cancer or syphilis, it is a private disaster that we discuss only reluctantly with our physician." Death is enveloped in secrecy. We whisper about it, and we whisper around the dying. Guided by a harsh independence, we are expected to handle the deaths of those close to us alone. We are also expected to face our own death as we are expected to face crises throughout our lives, alone.

The emphasis on hard work and achievement redefines death as something to be overcome by a great individual effort. Just as sex, according to Lewis and Brissett (1967) can only be dignified for Americans by turning it into a kind of work, so it is with dying. Just as sex requires hard work, practice, study, and scheduling, so too does dying. In a sense, dying becomes a final opportunity to succeed.

To die, then, is to fail. But even if the struggle is futile, at least a person can achieve the right kind of death (Charmaz, 1980:14), that is, to die in accordance with some model of what constitutes a proper style of dying.

Glaser and Strauss (1965:86) have described one such model, hospital patients' proper style of dying. Although these guidelines are hardly printed in the patients' handbook, they are nonetheless communicated to patients by the actions and attitudes of family, staff, and often other patients.

> The patient should maintain relative composure and cheerfulness. At the very least, he should face death with dignity. He should not cut himself off from the world, turning his back upon the living; instead he should continue to be a good family member, and be "nice" to other patients. If he can, he should participate in the ward social life. He should cooperate with the staff members who care for him, and if possible he should avoid distressing or embarrassing them.

SCIENCE AND THE MASTERY OF NATURE

To Americans, nature represents a challenge; nature is a force to be mastered. As John Spiegel (1964:291) expressed it, people are "expected to triumph in any contest with nature, in accordance with an optimistic confidence in the power of science and technology."

This faith shows up in many areas of American life. Although we know that industrial pollution has been one of the by-products of technological and scientific advance, we maintain confidence that further advances will eradicate that same pollution, for science giveth and science taketh away.

This faith finds its strongest expression in relation to health and medical research. In Zborowski's (1952:26) study of various ethnic groups' responses to pain, he describes the dominant American faith in science: "Patients with intractable pain often state that though at the present moment the doctors do not have the 'drug' they will eventually discover it, and they will give the examples of sulpha, penicillin, etc."

Medical research has produced cures and preventatives for many of the scourges of the past. Such research has extended life expectancy beyond the dreams of previous generations. Following this reasoning, why shouldn't the process continue until death itself is eradicated?

The cryogenics movement is the ultimate extension of this faith. Cryonics societies began forming in the mid-1960s after R. C. W. Ettinger (1966) suggested that corpses might be frozen and defrosted later when medicine had discovered a cure for what the person had "died" from (see Segerberg, 1974:89–90). Although the movement is small, it is based on a value that is widely subscribed to, albeit in less exaggerated form. But of course the fact that death resists technological solution, that as much as we stall it, we can never abolish it, makes death particularly hard for Americans to handle.

Death has come to be reconceptualized as a technological problem. Eric Cassell (1975:43–48) attributes the shift from a moral to a technological emphasis to several factors. These include the success medicine has had in postponing death. Technology has also succeeded in controlling other basic areas of human life, for example, birth. In addition, he claims, the elderly, "the repository of knowledge about what is right and the major recipients of moral obligation, have left the family group" (44). They more often live away from their families and less often die among them.

In general, the scene of dying has shifted to the institution. As Cassell (48) puts it,

> When death occurs in the modern hospital there seems to be more concern for the disease than for the dying person, more concern for life as a

succession of heartbeats than life as meaning. When death occurs in nursing homes it is as if life just dribbled out—custodial care seemingly inconvenienced by individual differences or tenacity for life.

This technological redefinition affects the treatment of the dying. The nurse's role is conceptualized as a technical one. Consequently, nurses are held accountable for the technical, but not for the emotional, care of patients. Anselm Strauss and Jeanne Quint (1964) call this, "the non-accountability of terminal care." In Jules Henry's (1963:406) powerful words,

> Society is satisfied that it has "done its best" when it pours oxygen into a dying man. That he has first been degraded to the level of social junk is none of its affair.

FUTURE ORIENTATION

Americans tend to be great believers in progress. This implies both an orientation toward the future and an optimism about it. It also tends to involve a disdain for the past. As Robin Williams (1960:432) points out, the negative connotation of terms like "old fashioned" and "outmoded" can only be understood "against the unquestioning assumption that the new is the better—that 'forward' is better than 'backward.' "

The belief in the future is so strong in American culture that for a time, the supposed inability of lower-class children to defer gratification (a process predicated on faith in future rewards) was regarded as a *pathological* consequence of being "culturally disadvantaged."

This future orientation creates a major problem in facing death. "In a culture that puts so much stress on the future, the prospect of not having any future at all becomes too dismal to face" (Spiegel, 1964:297). This partially accounts for the stigma that attaches to the elderly. For with the passage of time, a person's future grows shorter and shorter while their past grows longer and longer. As a 70-year-old student of mine once said, "At a certain point in my life, I began to look forward less and less and back more and more" (Kamerman, 1975). This is also the basis for the accusation young people sometimes make of the old, that all they want to do is talk about the past.

If their diminishing future represents a difficulty in dealing with the elderly, then the absence of a future is that much more difficult to handle in the dying. That may explain why a common tack in conversation with the dying is to talk about the future, whether on this earth, when it would be called denial, or in the afterlife, when it would be called faith. The elderly then bear the double stigma of being carriers of death and carriers of the past.

SOCIAL VALUATION AND THE TREATMENT OF DYING PATIENTS

There is another way that values intersect with death and dying. The social value of a patient in the eyes of the hospital staff affects their treatment of the patient, their reaction to the patient's death, and sometimes even the patient's chances for life.

Glaser and Strauss (1964) studied the impact on nurses of patients' deaths. A nurse may feel a *personal loss* to the extent that personal involvement has developed. This involvement may be based on a friendship, an identification formed with the patient, or on being the same age, or engaged in the same occupation, for example. A nurse may feel a *work loss* to the extent to which efforts have been made in vain to save the patient. Finally, a nurse may feel a *social loss* based on the patient's valued social characteristics.

The most important of these characteristics is age. Age even supersedes accomplishment. For example, the death of an 80-year-old religious leader may not have as much impact as the death of almost any 3-three-year-old child. Other social characteristics include beauty and charm, social class, skin color, talent, accomplishment, family status, occupation, and education (119).

In addition to the values used to calculate social loss, the nurse's reaction to a patient's death is influenced by professional values, for example, those that constrain personal involvement with patients, and by cultural values specifically related to death.

David Sudnow (1967a; 1967b) also studied the effects of patients' valued social characteristics. However, he focused on how these characteristics affect efforts to save the lives of those patients.

In studying the treatment of patients brought into the hospital's emergency room, Sudnow (1967a) observed that life-saving efforts tend to be made for high social value patients, for example, children, more often than for low social value patients. In addition to age and social background, the "perceived moral character of patients [affects] . . . the amount of effort that is made to attempt revival when 'clinical death signs' are detected (and, for that matter, the amount of effort given to forestalling their appearance in the first place)" (103).

The perceived moral characteristics of suicides, alcoholics, and dope addicts, for example, make it more likely that their "deaths will be more quickly judged, and . . . [their] 'dying' more readily noticed"

(105). As a consequence, Sudnow makes the biting recommendation that "If one anticipates having a critical heart attack, he had best keep himself well-dressed and his breath clean if there is a likelihood he will be brought into the County Emergency Unit as a 'possible' [DOA]" (105).

SUMMARY

Values exert an important influence on our attitudes and behavior toward death and dying. Four major American value themes were discussed.

The shift from a sacred to a secular view of death left Americans face to face with the finality of death. Two patterns developed in response, avoidance and denial. Some controversy surrounds the issue of the extent to which avoidance and denial continue to constitute the dominant American reaction to death. The most tenable position is to acknowledge that a shift has taken place toward a more direct confrontation with death, but that avoidance and denial still remain the dominant responses.

The values subsumed by the Protestant Ethos still exercise an important influence. Americans are expected to face death by themselves. Dying has become a final opportunity for achievement and success. The goal is to die well, and to do that, we are expected to work at dying.

Because Americans emphasize the mastery of nature and are oriented toward the future, death is particularly hard to accept. Death resists conquest by science and death represents the end of the future.

Finally, the relationship of values to death and dying can be seen in the way that valued social characteristics affect the treatment of the dying.

The position of the elderly in the United States can be understood if you measure them against this list of values. They are the carriers of death and are to be avoided because they make our denial of death more difficult. They often no longer work and so have been robbed of the principal basis for dignity in America, their occupations. They are "un-American" because they have limited futures. They are, ironically, both the principal keepers and victims of these values.

In Slawomir Mrozek's (1968:93–95) play *Tango*, the grandmother, Eugenia, announces that she is dying. The brother, Eugene, says, "This is ridiculous, Eugenia. Pull yourself together. This is no way to behave . . . this is carrying eccentricity too far. This sort of thing isn't done in our family." Her granddaughter, Ala, says, "It wouldn't be normal, Grandmother." Her son-in-law, Stomil, says, "It's sheer hypocrisy."

To her family, she replies, "I don't understand you people. You're all so intelligent, but if somebody wants to do something as simple as dying, you don't know what to make of it. Really, you are very strange people."

And when she dies, each in turn expresses a thread of the American response to death. Ala: "I can't stand it!" Eugene: "I don't understand it." Stomil: "I don't want to have anything to do with this."

Notes

1. This is not to say that denial is necessarily dysfunctional. For the functions of denial in general, see Dumont and Foss (1972:45). For the functions of denial for the dying, see Beilen (1981–82).

2. Avery Weisman (1977:111) has suggested that the public discussion of death over the past twenty-five years may have produced less a move toward acceptance than a greater difficulty in denying it. "It is more difficult to hide from death today. Perhaps that contributes to the feeling that we no longer 'deny' death."

CHAPTER FOUR
HOSPITALS, HOSPICES, AND "HOMES": INSTITUTIONAL SETTINGS FOR DYING AS A ROLE CAREER

TABLE 4-1 Proportion of Deaths by Place in New York City, 1967[a] and 1984[b]

Year	Total	Institutions	At Home	Other
1967				
Number:	87,610	64,083	21,222	2,305
Percentage:	100.0%	73.1%	24.2%	2.6%
1984				
Number:	74,278	56,179	15,549	2,550
Percentage:	100.0%	75.6%	20.9%	3.4%

[a]Data are from Lerner(1970:23).
[b]Data are from personal communication, Bureau of Health Statistics, New York City Department of Health, August 13, 1985.

To understand behavior, it must be situated, that is, located in relation to its larger historical and cultural context as well as to its more immediate setting. The same behavior in two different settings may have two different meanings. The relationship of death and dying to history and culture was discussed in the previous chapter. In this chapter, death and dying will be studied in their most common settings, institutions. The social organization of these institutions affects the way in which dying patients are treated by staff and the way in which patients experience their own dying.

Most Americans die in institutions. In 1949, 49.5 percent of deaths in the United States took place in institutions; by 1958, the rate had risen to 60.9 percent (Lerner, 1970:22). In 1982, 68.1 percent of the people who died in the United States died as in-patients in hospitals or other institutions.[1] From 1955 to 1967, in New York City, the proportion of people dying in institutions to those dying at home rose steadily. In 1955, 65.9 percent died in institutions, 73.1 percent in 1967 (Lerner, 1970:23). Table 4-1 indicates that the proportion dying in institutions continued to rise through 1984. Although a countertrend may be developing (Mor and Hiris, 1983:375–376), the overall picture remains the same.

To understand dying in the United States, it is necessary to examine the institutions in which it most often occurs. It will be helpful, first, to expand on the idea introduced in Chapter Two, that dying can be seen as a role career.

MODELS OF DYING CAREERS

Dying trajectories, the courses dying takes, have two dimensions: duration and shape (Glaser and Strauss, 1968: 5–6). They last a certain amount of time and they follow one of several patterns. People may die over a long period of time (*lingering trajectories*) or may die quickly (*quick-dying trajectories*). Staff may expect someone to die in a short time, and he or she may ("expected quick death"). Staff may expect a patient to die, but not as quickly as it happens ("unexpected quick dying, but expected to die"). Finally, staff may not expect a patient to die, but death comes suddenly ("unexpected quick dying, not expected to die") (Strauss and Glaser, 1970a:133–134).

Different trajectories have different consequences for family, staff, and institution. Hospitals, Glaser and Strauss (1970:133) point out, are set up to handle quick trajectories rather than lingering ones. Nursing homes, on the other hand, can also accommodate lingering trajectories. In fact, as Gubrium (1976:86–87) points out, from the patient's point of view admission to a nursing home may be seen as the beginning of "dying."

Lingering trajectories may allow both family and staff to prepare better for the patient's death. On the other hand, anticipatory grieving may create a guilt-ridden distance between family and patient by the time of death (Fulton and Fulton, 1971). A lingering illness may involve expenses and inconvenience that generate resentment in the family toward the patient. The consequences of quick-dying trajectories are the mirror images of those of lingering trajectories with additional questions raised in the minds of family if the patient dies unexpectedly.

Another approach to the dying role careers is the attempt to arrange them in stages. The most popular and also the most widely criticized stage model was advanced by Elisabeth Kübler-Ross (1969) in her book, *On Death and Dying*. She posits five stages through which a patient may pass in the course of dying: denial and isolation, anger, bargaining, depression, and acceptance. Although she acknowledges that a patient may not pass through all five and that some patients may backslide into an earlier stage, the basic idea of her model is that these five stages represent a sequence, in fact, the typical sequence. These stages are both a *descriptive sequence* of what happens to a dying patient and a *set of therapeutic recommendations* because those who work with dying patients are commended to see the patient's acceptance as a therapeutic goal (Kübler-Ross, 1969:119–120). Her model is prescriptive in another sense: professionals using this model may interpret a patient's behavior in terms of these stages and then act toward patients in ways to make these stages a reality; that is, the model may become a self-fulfilling prophecy. This is an excellent example of the process of social construction discussed in Chapter Two. As Kathy Charmaz (1980:153), perhaps the most effective critic in sociology of

Kübler-Ross's work, wrote, "What originated as *description* of reality often becomes *prescription* for reality."

As a descriptive sequence, Kübler-Ross's work has been subjected to two basic criticisms: (1) that with regard to the *interpretations of the five stages in her model,* what she has observed is subject to other equally plausible interpretations (Charmaz, 1976; 1980), and (2) that her *basic model is inaccurate,* that patients' reactions don't fall into stages at all, still less five of them (Shneidman, 1973:3–23).

Some of Kübler-Ross's stages are open to equally, if not more, plausible interpretations. Denial, as Charmaz (1980:149–150) points out, rests on the imposition of a professional's interpretation (and often judgment) of a patient's behavior and future. Kübler-Ross (1969:42–45) discusses the case of a woman who was terminally ill, went to a faith healer, and became "inappropriately cheerful" and opti- mistic. While in that case denial is an appropriate judgment (the patient died), its *categorical* use in all cases where physicians predict death is hardly warranted.[2] She also fails to give sufficient weight to the staff's part in promoting the denial of death by patients. As Hans O. Mauksch points out, "The hospital and its personnel tend to reward the patient for maintaining the denial phase because it protects the hospital personnel from becoming involved and from facing their own feelings" (1975:10).

Anger, Kübler-Ross contends, is "really" about the unfairness of dying, but is displaced on family and staff. Charmaz (1980:150–151) claims that the anger may be a response to staff anger directed at the patient for interfering with their routine. This, of course, is true to an extent for all hospital patients.

Bargaining, Kübler-Ross claims, is made with God to postpone death. On the other hand, bargaining is a normal feature of institutional life (Roth, 1963:30–59; Goffman, 1961:171–320). Bargaining may be for amenities or some semblance of control in the midst of the constraints and indignities of a patient's daily life. Gustafson (1972) points to another possible goal of bargaining, to postpone the definition by staff and family of the patient as a nonperson, that is, as being as good as dead. She acknowledges that in the terminal phase, patients may in fact bargain with God for more time. But even then, there is no reason to assume that they give up the need to be treated as still-living persons.

In sum, as Charmaz maintains, Kübler-Ross's stages of dying, to the extent that they accurately reflect the elements, if not the sequence, of patients' reactions to death, may be a consequence more of institutional demands, staff needs, and cultural values than of any universal human destiny.

Edwin Shneidman (1973:3–23) criticizes Kübler-Ross's work in a second way. He claims that although he has seen in dying patients the emotions and behaviors that characterize her "stages," they didn't occur in any necessary sequence, but rather in an undulating jumble, that is, in combinations of feelings more or less prominent for longer or shorter durations. He claims that both the model of stages and the positing of their universality simply aren't accurate.

The stages of dying are also a set of therapeutic recommendations. Acceptance is not simply the last stage, according to Kübler-Ross, but the goal of working with dying patients. Whether this goal is admirable is a value question outside the scope of sociological analysis. It is appropriate, however, to examine the functions of adopting acceptance as a goal.

One consequence is the tacit approval (or at least the lack of disapproval) of the justness of a death. For example, Charmaz (1980:153) mentions the case described by Kübler-Ross (1970:161–165) of a poor black woman with kidney failure who was turned down for dialysis at the only two hospitals in her area with dialysis units servicing the poor. As Charmaz points out, while the patient was emotionally propped up, the underlying reasons she was brought to the point of death in the first place were pushed into the background. In the terms of C. Wright Mills (1959:8), focusing on her *troubles* meant a failure to focus on the *issues* that created these troubles in the first place. Whether this is a therapist's job or not is, of course, a separate question.

Another consequence of bringing a patient to acceptance is that it makes for a more manageable patient (Charmaz, 1980:154). (Imagine, for example, the effect on ward life of recommending that patients be brought to and left at the stage of anger.) The stages of dying also bring a sense of orderliness to an often disorderly process, dying. They function as an *ideology* (a set of ideas used to justify a group's actions), justifying uniform treatment of a collection of individuals. (Again, imagine the alternative: tailoring each dying course to each individual patient.) They allow the distance that comes from being analytical toward an emotion-saturated event. With one model making both patients and their deaths easier to handle, it is small wonder that Kübler-Ross's work, in spite of these long-standing criticisms, is so popular in professional programs.[3] In medical school courses on death, for example, "For required reading the author most frequently cited is Elisabeth Kübler-Ross" (Dickinson, 1981:112).

In sum, however great are Kübler-Ross's understanding of dying, contributions to the popularization of the subject, and therapeutic insights (and they are all considerable), as a social scientific analysis of what actually happens to dying patients, her work has major flaws.

DYING IN A TOTAL INSTITUTION: CONSEQUENCES FOR IDENTITY

The settings for dying discussed in this chapter are *total institutions,* institutions in which people live twenty-four hours a day (Goffman, 1961:1–124). Although there are several types, for example, those that stigmatize (prisons) and those that don't (boarding schools), they have in common that a person's life, for however long they reside there, is lived within the walls of the institution.[4] Total institutions to one degree or another cut inmates off from the outside world and consequently subject them to the confines of institutional rules.

What does dying in a total institution represent in terms of identity? The question is really two questions strung together: (1) What does dying represent in terms of identity? and (2) What does being in a total institution represent in terms of identity?

Death and Identity

As Robert Fulton (1976:3) so clearly phrased it,

Death asks us for our identity. Confronted by death, man is compelled to provide in some form a response to the question: Who am I? the manner in which this question has been asked and the replies that it has received have varied from era to era and have reflected the personal aspirations and the social consensus of the time and place. It is only the implacable and challenging presence of death itself which has remained constant.

As discussed in Chapter Two, all role careers have a retroactive character. In fact, a person's overall sense of self has a similar character. George Herbert Mead (1932) suggested that a person's sense of self at a given moment is an amalgam of the past as it is seen at that moment and the possibilities ("possible futures") that lie ahead. The past is reworked over and over again as the present keeps changing. If you consider yourself a good student because you have a B average and then fail a course, you will likely reassess your quality as a student in light of this new evidence. You might, for example, say, "A B average means the F is unusual, and I'll get back on the track next term. *Conclusion:* I continue to be the good student I was in the past and I'll prove it again next term." Or, you might say, "I received an F in the only tough course I've taken so far, so the B average doesn't mean very much. The courses coming up will also be tough; this is the beginning of the end of my grade point average. *Conclusion:* I thought I was a good student, but I 'really' wasn't. I'm pretty bad, as the D's and F's that lie ahead will prove."

The power of death is that it represents the final chance to rework and retitle the events of your life. It is the final summing-up, quite literally the last word on the self. Although belief in an afterlife provides some with a possible future, death is, for all, the final version of the self in this life. There are no future opportunities to make up for present failings. That obduracy makes it unlike any other point in a person's life.

Total Institutions and Identity

To be in a total institution is to be cut off to one degree or another from the moorings of an outside identity. You are removed from familiar people, places, and props. Inmates, according to Goffman (1961), undergo a process of mortification in which the institution strips away their sense of self by means of isolation and homogenization. In a general hospital, for example, your clothes are taken away, you're put into a uniform (hospital dressing gown), you're put into a room like all the other hospital rooms, given an identity wristband, put on an institutional schedule, and in many other ways told that whatever you were on the outside, in the hospital, you're just a patient.[5] Of course, outside identities impinge on insider status; for example, a hospital patient who is also a physician on the staff of that hospital will likely be accorded better treatment than will the average patient. And some institutions, particularly those where your stay is short, where (unlike mental hospitals in which your very ability to make judgments is called into question) your sense of things carries some weight, and where the barriers to the outside world are permeable, stand less of a chance of stripping away your identity. But even in those milder total institutions, you need reminders of the imminence of the outside world, particularly after the lights go out or if your stay turns out to be longer than you expected.

By taking away a person's "identity kit" (Goffman, 1961:20–21), an institution puts his or her sense of self in jeopardy. When patients are free-floating, the institution imposes its own version of identity on them. This is done very effectively in some cases, for example, long-term stays in mental hospitals and years-long hostage situations, and less effectively in others, for example, short-term stays in general hospitals.

Dying in a Total Institution

The consequences for identity of dying in a total institution are a combination of the consequences of dying and of being in a total institution. Death confronts you with the obliteration of the self. If the institution also makes your identity problematic, the journey into the unknown becomes much more ominous. You are unsure of where you are going, and even worse, *who* is going. If you die in a total institution that stigmatizes, for example, a prison, your identity becomes less problematic, but more terrible. This "prisoner" is the final version of the self. In that sense, each person's dying day is Judgment Day.

THE SOCIAL ORGANIZATION OF INSTITUTIONS: CONSEQUENCES FOR THE TREATMENT OF DYING PATIENTS

The treatment of dying patients in institutions stems from the fact that they are *dying* and from the fact that they are *patients*. To some extent, dying constitutes a special state with special treatment associated with it. However, the treatment of dying patients is also an extension of the treatment of all patients.

As you would expect, values that define death in American society color the reaction of institutional staff to dying patients. Death also represents failure to professionals whose central goals are the preservation of life and the conquest of disease. Cure remains the goal of medical treatment, even when it is clear that a patient's death is inevitable. In a study of dying patients in a teaching hospital, Mumma and Benoliel (1984–85:285) found that "Despite the fact that the majority of patients had been designated no code [no resuscitation attempts to be made] and had conditions labeled by their physicians as either grim or terminal, the treatment orientation was overwhelmingly toward the cure end of the comfort-cure continuum."

This tendency to define a patient in terms of the criteria for measuring successful professional work is only one example of a more common phenomenon.[6] "Good" patients are patients who make professionals look good, just as "good" students are students who make teachers look good. Part of making professionals look good is appreciating the reasons why they fail to do their jobs when that occurs, for example, a patient acknowledging that a nurse is overworked and so not complaining about slow service. Mauksch (1975:11) quotes a head nurse's tearful characterization of a patient as "cooperative": "Do you know how cooperative she really was? She even committed suicide exactly at three o'clock, so that neither shift would have to be responsible for the consequences."

When a patient is pronounced dying, staff visits and attention tend to diminish (Hackett and Weisman, 1964:308), particularly when a patient makes it clear that the staff's efforts are in vain (Glaser and Strauss, 1968:92–93). Mauksch (1975:14) suggests that a death is especially disruptive on wards where death is uncommon, for example, obstetrics, and the trajectory sudden. The possibility that someone made a mistake is raised:

> The unanticipated death not only upset everyone and created an aura of guilt and failure, but it tended to serve as a conflict-creating event among people involved in the care of this patient. Communications diminished, and it was obvious that following the death of that patient nobody trusted anybody else. (14)

All the behaviors just discussed follow in the main from a patient's being classified as dying. However, much of the treatment of dying patients has to do with their being patients. Hospital patients are subjected to at least two sets of forces. (1) Hospitals are *organizations* and may have organizational goals separate from and sometimes in conflict with their goals as treatment centers. (2) Hospitals are bureaucratically organized and have characteristics common to all *bureaucracies.*[7]

Hospitals are treatment centers, research facilities, and teaching institutions. They are also organizations. A hospital may do things to enhance its reputation, solidify its economic position, and so on, that conflict with its goals as a treatment center. For example, a hospital may build a treatment unit or acquire a piece of equipment such as a CAT scan unit because of the prestige involved rather than the need in the community the hospital services. Greater prestige may be one result, but underutilization may be another.

Other service organizations are subject to the same conflicting goals. Colleges, for example, may institute some programs and abandon others in response to fashions in education rather than educational value. They may also take administrative measures for economic reasons—for instance, increasing class size to reduce faculty—that conflict with educational goals.

The stage for the playing out of this conflict is the bureaucratic structure that houses both administrators and professionals. Although the term *dual authority* (Smith, 1955) is usually used to describe this bureaucratic feature in relation to hospitals, the friction it describes is common to most bureaucracies in which professionals are housed.[8] The problem for nurses and other professional employees is that while loyalties are to the profession and the standards of good professional practice, the administration, rather than the American Nursing Association, promotes nurses on administrative grounds. As Freidson

(1973:22–24) points out, while professionals in organizations like hospitals tend to control the work, they tend to control the job less successfully. Consequently, in situations of choice between satisfying professional and organizational demands, the latter usually prevail.

Bureaucracies, because they are organizations designed to operate efficiently and rationally (in Max Weber's sense, that is, predictably or according to calculable rules), are run on schedules. Strauss and Glaser (1970a) point to the discrepancy between staff schedules and patients' inner clocks. "The staff operates on 'work time.' Their tasks are guided by schedules usually related to many patients, both dying and recovering" (146). When patients become dying patients, they move off that time track to one with a truncated future and a self-consciously recapitulated past. A consequence of this dissonance between senses of time, according to Glaser and Strauss, may be a patient's increasing isolation.

Dying patients are fit into hospital work schedules as are all other patients. In the case of dying patients, physicians must predict the length of time a dying patient has left to live. Bad predictions of both sorts, underestimating or overestimating time left, can have serious consequences for staff and family. For staff, the trajectory of dying affects the allocation of resources, "so that manpower will not be withdrawn suddenly from other patients nor the scheduling of tasks with them disrupted" (Glaser and Strauss, 1968:13). For family, underestimating the duration of dying may allow little preparation for death, and overestimating may produce families assembling for a death watch prematurely, then scattering again to distant homes. Overestimating may also produce anticipatory grief and its accompanying guilt.

Death is also fit into work schedules. Sudnow (1967a:82) says that it was common at the hospital he studied for aides or orderlies to ignore or even prop up patients who died toward the end of a shift. "If they succeed, aides or orderlies can manage to pass off the body for the next shift, which, when rounds are made, will discover it and be responsible for wrapping it."

Impersonality is a feature of all bureaucracies. It is intended to ensure the impartial treatment of people serviced by an organization. The rules of an organization help to produce this impartiality. But what works to ensure the fair treatment of customers on line at a bank may have very different consequences for patients dying in a hospital. Impersonality may be interpreted by patients as depersonalization, often with justification. Patients may be seen merely as specific cases of general rules. As Hackett and Weisman (1964:300) observe, "In a large general hospital, where numerous deaths occur in the course of a day, it is almost impossible to find a dying patient who is allowed to respond to the imminence of death in his own way." Dying patients, perhaps to a greater degree than other patients, have diminishing control over their circumstances, particularly the more physically debilitated they become. They are less able to resist the pressure of hospital structure. And, as Freidson (1970b:170) notes, *"Depersonalitization is most marked when the client is most helpless, when the choice and arrangement of services are an exclusive prerogative of management."*

SETTINGS FOR DYING

Nursing Homes and Old Age Homes

Death is an everyday occurrence in old age homes and nursing homes. The administrative policies of those institutions are an important factor in the dying role careers of residents. Victor Marshall (1976) studied dying in an old age home, St. Joseph's, and a retirement community, Glen Brae. He found that the major difference between the two was the degree to which residents had control over the course of their dying. In St. Joseph's, dying was structured by a formal administrative policy. Residents defined as dying were moved from dormitory to infirmary to St. Peter's Room, the "dying room." In Glen Brae, by contrast, the community of residents informally worked out their own approach to handling dying and death. Funerals and funeral services were similarly standardized at St. Joseph's and individualized at Glen Brae.

Marshall concludes that these two styles of control and the differing senses of community on which they are predicated have different consequences for the legitimation of death. At Glen Brae, in sharp contrast to St. Joseph's, residents tended to accept their deaths and the deaths of others as appropriate. "Perhaps the greatest evidence of such legitimation lies in the ease with which residents [of Glen Brae] could formulate thoughts about death and dying—including their own—to me as an investigator" (Marshall, 1975:1126).

Elizabeth Gustafson (1972) writes that the careers of most nursing home patients point toward death from the time of admission. Interaction between patients is inhibited by the fact that, contrary to popular categorizing, residents may have nothing in common except old age. She focuses on bargaining as a crucial career process. Bargaining is initially an attempt to fend off the judgment of social death by staff and family. She calls this the social phase of the career. When death is imminent, which she calls the terminal phase, the goal of bargaining is to fend off clinical death. This bargaining can be seen as an attempt to get some grip on those few aspects of death, a basically uncontrollable process, that can be manipulated. In an institution such as St. Joseph's, which controls living as well as dying, a sense of help-lessness is almost unavoidable.

Hospitals

The situation of dying patients in a general hospital has also been marked traditionally by a lack of control over the circumstances of their daily lives and the course of their dying. Some of this lack of con-trol has to do with the specific nature of each terminal illness. Some, as suggested earlier in this chapter, has to do with hospital structure.

One way of tracking the features of hospital structure that influ-ence the dying hospital patient's role is to focus on the conditions that support two of the awareness contexts described by Glaser and Strauss (1965), closed awareness and suspicion awareness. (These contexts were introduced in Chapter Two as examples of the influence of defini-tions of the situation on interaction between staff and dying patients.)

Several structural conditions support closed awareness. Hospi-tals are set up to deny patients access to information about their condi-tion. Records are kept at a distance from patients. Discussion of a pa-tient's condition also takes place at a distance, or, if it is within earshot, in medical jargon that constitutes an equally effective barrier. In addition, most patients aren't medically sophisticated and cannot tell when they've moved from very sick to dying. Finally, "The patient has no allies who reveal or help him discover the staff's knowledge of his impending death. Not only his family but other patients withhold information, if they know" (32).

Closed awareness tends to be unstable because of the inexorable progress of terminal illnesses and, in some cases, because of the failure of organizational efficiency, for example, the staff failing from one shift to another to maintain a consistent posture toward a patient (Glaser and Strauss, 1965:39–40).

Suspicion awareness is often a consequence of a deterioration of the conditions supporting closed awareness. Suspicion awareness re-flects in part the conditions that produce closed awareness (otherwise closed awareness would always move directly to open awareness). In addition, the rules of organizational efficiency just mentioned and the fact that hospital patients ordinarily expect to be put off and lied to encourage suspicion awareness. Patients may attempt to breach secu-rity by peeking at charts or asking a doctor or nurse directly, not anticipating honesty, but hope to "read" the truth in their faces (53).

In sum, the hospital controls to a great extent the daily lives of dying patients, as well as the information that might alter the mean-ing of their dying.

Hospices

Partly in response to the predicament of patients dying in the restrictive atmosphere of traditional institutions, the hospice was developed. St. Christopher's, the first hospice for the care of dying patients, was opened in London by Dr. Cicely Saunders in 1967. Its goals included not simply humanization of the care of the dying in hospices but the spread of hospice principles to other institutions in which people die. As Dr. Saunders (1977) described it,

> It was planned to be something between a hospital and the patient's own home; combining the skills of the one with the warmth and welcome, the time available, and the beds without invisible parking meters beside them of the other. (160)

Hospice programs in the United States take a number of forms, for example, hospice units within general hospitals, hospice teams that service dying patients in all wards of a hospital, home care programs, and so on (Backer, Hannon, and Russell, 1982:68–71). The National Hospice Organization estimates that about a thousand hospice programs, encompassing all these various types, were operating in the United States by 1985 in varying stages of development.[9]

Hospice programs have run into enormous legal and financial difficulties as well as into opposition from more traditional health care programs in seeking to become established. This is a frequent concomitant of the growth of radical movements in health care. (Of course, that humane treatment of dying patients should constitute a radical approach is an interesting barometer of current conditions.) The hospice threatens traditional health care programs precisely because it demands that they bend in its direction. As Koff (1980) puts it,

> There is current recognition that hospice care must be closely related to the mainstream of health care activity in order to exist and have maximum impact on care of the dying person, not only to avoid the "house of death" stigma, but also to make an important statement regarding the direction health care as a whole should take. (172)

In spite of significant differences in philosophy between traditional and hospice programs for care of the dying, hospices are also organizations and as such are subject to some of the same constraints as organizations discussed earlier in this chapter. So, for example, Mor and Hiris (1983) found that bed availability in the hospices they studied was the major factor determining whether dying cancer patients were sent home to die (the philosophic preference of many in the hospice movement) or kept in the hospice unit to die. This was to only some extent explained by whether or not the hospice was hospital affiliated or had control over its own operations. In general, Mor and Hiris concluded,

> It seems that the same organizational factors that bias decisions regarding the conventional-care patient's site of death are also at work in determining where the hospice patient will die, that is, the need to fill beds, ease of access for the patient's doctor, etc. (384)

SUMMARY

Dying, as all behavior, must be understood in relation to the setting in which it occurs. In this chapter, the major institutional settings for dying were examined.

Dying is a role. When people die over a period of time, they have careers in that role. Dying careers follow different patterns or trajectories. One conceptualization of the dying career is the stages of dying advanced by Elisabeth Kübler-Ross. This model was criticized as both a description and a set of therapeutic recommendations. Kübler-Ross's observations are susceptible to equally, if not more, plausible interpretations. Some have claimed that her very model, stages, doesn't reflect the reality of dying patients' reactions. Her therapeutic recommendations function to make for a manageable patient and fit neatly with some of the ideological assumptions of the health care professions.

Since the settings discussed in this chapter are total institutions, the concept was examined, specifically the total institution's effects on an inmate's sense of self. Total institutions tend to first strip away old identities and then impose institutional identities on inmates. They do this with varying degrees of effectiveness. Since death forces a final confrontation with our selves, and total institutions place our sense of self in jeopardy, dying in a total institution can have powerful consequences for an inmate's emotional life.

The treatment of dying patients is the sum of the consequences of *being dying* and *being a patient*. Some of the characteristics of hospitals as organizations were analyzed. Hospitals are organizations, and their goals as organizations may conflict with their goals as treatment centers. Hospitals are most often bureaucratically organized. This fact alone explains aspects of the treatment of patients. Bureaucracies are impersonal, run on schedules, and are subject to conflicts between administrative and professional staff.

We are all helpless in an ultimate sense in the face of death. This helplessness is compounded by the extent to which various institutions, nursing homes, hospitals, and to a lesser extent, hospices, usurp control over the lives of patients, even as their lives ebb away.

The missing element in the institutions discussed in this chapter has been the personnel who populate them. They will be discussed in the next chapter.

Notes

1. For the forty-two states tabulated. Personal communication from the Division of Vital Statistics, National Center for Health Statistics, Hyattsville, Md., August 13, 1985.

2. An interesting example of that error in reverse is found in the cases analyzed by Avery Weisman and Thomas P. Hackett (1961) in their study, "Predilection to Death." In each case, the patient was convinced of impending death although in some cases efforts were made by professionals to dispel that "pessimism," a realistic "pessimism," since all patients, in fact, died.

3. In addition to the consequences already mentioned, in a few cases, bringing a patient to acceptance, that is, helping to abandon the struggle against death, may bring death sooner. This is similar to the consequences of being defined as socially dead discussed in Chapter Two.

4. This is an *ideal type* (a model against which reality is measured). Real institutions are more or less but not necessarily perfectly "total." A mental hospital may be "total" for some patients. Others may leave the grounds by day to work and return to sleep at night. The institution's control tends to vary with the degree of access (physical or otherwise) to the outside world.

5. Coe (1978:330–335) calls the components of this process in a general hospital *stripping, control of resources,* and *restriction of mobility.*

6. Robert Faulkner (1973) makes the same point about orchestra musicians' evaluations of conductors.

7. There are, of course, other factors that influence the treatment of dying patients, for example, the process of social valuation discussed in Chapter Three. The occupations involved in health care are professions or are in the process of professionalization. This also affects patient care and will be discussed in Chapter Five. The emphasis, however, is on the structural factors related to the institutional settings where dying takes place.

8. Celia Davies (1983) has recommended that those who study bureaucracies should "abandon once and for all notions such as professional bureaucratic conflict" (192). What she demonstrates, however, is that professional–bureaucratic conflict is neither inevitable nor the only source of strain in bureaucratic settings. The concept still has utility.

9. Personal communication from the National Hospice Organization, Arlington, Va., August 19, 1985.

CHAPTER FIVE
THE HEALTH CARE PROFESSIONS AND THE MANAGEMENT OF DEATH AND DYING

The occupations that constitute the division of labor in health care are professions to one degree or another. Their status as professions influences the manner of their work, including their care and treatment of the dying. In this chapter, the consequences for the treatment of dying patients of professional status and would-be professional status are discussed. First, it is necessary to delineate the concept of *profession*.

PROFESSIONALIZATION AND ITS CONSEQUENCES

Profession has meant many things to many sociologists (Freidson, 1983). A number of theoretical controversies swirl around its definition. For the sake of simplicity and because it also seems the most useful definition for understanding the arrangement of occupations in health care, professions, as Eliot Freidson (1970a:77–84) points out, are occupations that have been granted legitimate control over their own work, that is, given a monopoly over a certain territory. In Freidson's view, they are granted this monopoly, often only after strenuous political struggles, not necessarily because they have certain characteristics, for example, a service ideal, but because they have been able to convince people with power (state legislatures, for example) that they have those characteristics. So, traits such as a service ideal and a distinct body of abstract knowledge are less important as realities than as arguments in a process of persuasion. As Arlene Kaplan Daniels (1973:56) puts it,

> What professions say about themselves in justification of their privileged status above ordinary occupations might better be studied as political ideology than as an indicator of intrinsic differences between professions and other types of occupations.

Designation as a profession, or, more precisely, the monopoly that such a designation symbolizes, means more income, more prestige, and more control. When occupations try to become professions, they try to evidence a service ideal, usually by establishing a code of ethics. They also try to establish the claim to a body of abstract knowledge, usually by locating their training programs in institutions of higher learning. Finally, they use their professional associations to try to establish a legal monopoly over a certain territory through licensing that controls entry into a field, through controlling training, and so forth.

An occupation's status as a profession and the quest of occupations for professional status have a number of consequences. Codes of ethics usually include a commitment never to do things in the interest of the professional at the expense of the client or patient. Ethical codes

also mean that professionals can claim to be above petty consumer–business considerations while at the same time conducting
thriving businesses.

While the development of a body of abstract knowledge and the
standardization of professionals' training in that knowledge provide
the basis for a consistent and high-quality service, they also have other
consequences. For one thing, they constitute a rationale for less ac-
countability. Professionals claim to be the only ones who understand
their own work and consequently the only ones capable of judging mistakes (Freidson, 1973:33). Passing a licensing examination means
that, on paper at least, so to speak, a minimal level of competence can
be assumed of any practitioner. But licensing also has the latent function of controlling the supply of practitioners, that is, of manipulating
the market.

Professionalization often means a shift of "dirty work" to lower
occupational levels. This may entail, as it did with nursing, the loss of
some tasks involving human contact and comfort. As Sam Schulman
(1979:279) phrased it, "Many of these functions seem to be 'dirty work'
beyond the pale of professionals."

Professional ideologies commit physicians and nurses to cure as
opposed to care. As mentioned in Chapter Four, this often promotes the
use of extraordinary means to sustain life even when dying seems inevitable. The outcome may be costly, futile, and, in some cases, contrary to the wishes of patient and family. Ideologies also support the
idea that involvement with patients not only drains the professional
emotionally, but equates with a loss of objectivity and a consequent inability to render service. As with all ideologies, the truth of these ideas
is never the question; their usefulness in justifying work practices is
their ultimate measure. Ideologies, which are learned in professional
schools and honed in work settings, are usually accepted on faith.

The force of the ideology of noninvolvement, combined as it is
with work that makes great emotional demands, promotes *emotional
reserve* as one trait of the *working personality* of professionals in health
care. Working personalities are emotional configurations produced in
response to the nature of specific kinds of work (Skolnick, 1975:42–70).
It is difficult to separate the traits produced by a certain kind of work
from prior personality traits that predisposed someone to enter the
kind of work for which he or she would be temperamentally suited.
However, by describing work conditions and their likely consequences,
you can understand at the very least the preexisting traits that will be
reinforced, the ones that will be troublesome, and so on.

Because physicians sit on top of the division of labor in health
care (Freidson, 1970b), *dominance* has marked the working personal-

ity of physicians and a complementary *obedience* has marked the working personality of nurses. Both physicians and nurses have traditionally dominated their relations with patients.

The conditions that produce working personalities are not, of course, static. The subservience of nurses to physicians has diminished in the past twenty years. A study done in 1966 (Hofling et al.) indicated that nurses would be willing to follow orders from physicians even if those orders contradicted hospital rules and good professional judgment. A similar study done ten years later (Rank and Jacobson, 1977) produced a very different result. Nurses were less willing to comply blindly with physicians' orders. Reasons offered by Rank and Jacobson for the change included, "The decrease in the status of doctors, [and] the increase in self-esteem of nurses" (193). The relationship between physicians and patients has also shifted to a more equalitarian basis.

In spite of these changes in the conditions that influence working personalities in health care, the hospital professional still often seems cold and authoritarian to patients operating at less than full strength. If these traits affect all patients, they certainly influence the morale of dying patients.

PHYSICIANS AND DEATH

Death is wound into the career choices and career paths of physicians. Some research suggests that attitudes toward death influence the choice of medicine as a career as well as the choice of specialties within medicine. These choices in turn interact with death attitudes. Death is also an important theme in professional socialization, both formal and informal.

Occupational Choice and Specialization

In a 1963 study, Herman Feifel suggested that "one of the major reasons certain physicians enter medicine is to govern their above-average fears concerning death" (1963:15). Feifel claimed that physicians' fears of death lay at the base of the resistance he encountered in gaining access to patients for a study of their attitudes toward death. A follow-up study in 1967 found the same result: among the reasons for choosing a medical career, for example, to help others, or to pursue a scientific interest in illness, was an above-average fear of death (Feifel et al., 1967). The choice of medicine with its emphasis on cure, the fending off of death, might be an attempt to neutralize these fears.

The study suggested that these fears also affect the treatment of dying patients. At precisely the moment when patients' needs are greatest, physicians may withdraw emotionally from them to avoid a confrontation with their own fears of death. This tendency is reinforced by the professional ideology of detachment.

More recently, Schulz and Aderman (1978–79) found that dying patients of physicians who experienced high death anxiety were kept alive in the hospital about five days longer than were those patients of physicians who experienced low or medium death anxiety. In contrast, the length of hospital stay of nondying patients had no relationship to the death anxiety of their physicians. While Schulz and Aderman view these results cautiously, their findings do "suggest that physicians' behaviors may be subtly influenced by personal attributes" (331). Again, "personal attributes" are reinforced by ideology, in this case, the ideology of cure as opposed to care.

The choice of specialization within medicine may also be influenced by attitudes toward death (Glaser and Strauss, 1965:5). Since different specialists have conspicuously different contact with death (e.g., allergists versus oncologists), it seems likely that this plays some part in the selection of a specialty. In addition, several studies have indicated that the more likely a medical specialist is to encounter death, the more comfortable the physician is in discussing it with patients (Rea, Greenspoon, and Spilka, 1975; Dickinson and Pearson, 1979a). What isn't clear is the extent to which these death attitudes are produced by or simply reinforced by the specialties chosen (Dickinson and Pearson, 1979a:685). In either case, the consequences for the treatment of dying patients are indisputable.

Professional Socialization

Writing in 1970, Rabin and Rabin claimed that "the medical profession seems to have little interest in the consequences of death for physicians, other medical personnel, and medical institutions" (186). This was reflected in the virtual absence of formal death education in medical schools.

By 1981, the situation had changed, but only somewhat. Comparing his 1975 and 1980 surveys of death education in American medical schools, Dickinson (1981) found that "While the limited offerings of occasional lectures and short 'mini' courses stayed the same (80 percent had such in 1975 and 1980), the number of full-term courses increased from 7 [of 107] to 16 [of 123] and those with no formal death education decreased from 14 to 10" (111–112). Taking a course in death seems to be related to greater rapport with dying patients and their families (Dickinson and Pearson, 1980–81). If death education currently represents an incidental part of medical school programs and if physicians who graduated from medical schools earlier than ten or fifteen years ago probably had no formal death education, then in most cases physicians' attitudes toward death would seem to reflect a combination of American values and the remainder of their professional socialization.[1]

Formal death education is obviously only a small part of professional socialization. Coombs and Powers (1976) studied the typical sequence of changes in attitudes toward death that physicians go through during medical school and early practice. While they acknowledge that this career path isn't necessarily followed by all medical students, it does represent the stages that "typically occur as laymen change into seasoned clinical practitioners" (17).

There are five developmental stages in their career model (18–32). In the first stage, which they call *idealizing the doctor's role,* students share the attitudes toward death of society at large. They see physicians as front-line soldiers in the battle against death and disease. Students identify with patients and consequently resent what they perceive as the coldness of the "case-hardened clinician" (18). Intellectually, on the other hand, students may realize that detachment doesn't mean unconcern and "may be in the best interests of the patient" (19).

In the second stage, *desensitizing death symbols,* students develop a blasé attitude about the signifiers of death. During the first year of medical school, the displacement of the initial horror at the prospect of dissecting a cadaver with a nonchalance in its presence is a barometer of this change. Getting through the first autopsy, that is, the confrontation with a near-person who was alive only hours before, is a major hurdle of the second year. To keep their balance in the face of death, medical students emulate the scientific attitude of their teachers. This ability to adopt an impersonal stance in situations that would normally call out strong personal feelings has been called *active dehumanization* (Silver and Geller, 1978).[2]

In the third stage, *objectifying and combatting death,* medical students generalize this scientific stance from corpses to dying patients. One technique is to focus on the pathological organ rather than on the person of whom it is a part. Death is seen as the symbol of professional failure. As Coombs and Powers (1976:25) put it, "No wonder a sense of personal defeat is felt when patients die."

As clinical experience is acquired, some physicians become disenchanted with this view of death and dying patients. In this fourth stage, *questioning the medical model,* physicians make some concessions to the overriding inevitability of death. "As physicians at this stage view it, 'the God complex' is incompatible with good medical practice" (28). Sensitivity to the needs of patient and family begins to ascend as the inflexible need to win over death begins to wane.

Finally, in the fifth stage, *dealing with personal feelings,* avoidance and suppression begin to give way to self-examination. Although Coombs and Powers make no claims about the likelihood of a physician's reaching this stage, they do point out that the relative lack of formal death education and the continuing ideological rewards for aloofness militate against it (31). So in effect this last stage represents more a goal than an achievement.

NURSES AND DEATH

Nursing as a Profession

Nursing is an occupation straining toward indisputable professional status; it is, in its self-defined mission, a would-be profession. As discussed, this quest for professional status is at base a process of persuasion. The definition of a unique body of knowledge becomes a central task in professionalization (Freidson, 1970a:80). As a leading textbook claimed

> As nursing has developed in professionalism, nursing scholars have developed theories of nursing, and the science of nursing is coming of age. A theoretical base of practice defines nursing's uniqueness; that is, it has a science of its own and is not simply an extension of another profession. (Kelly, 1981:161).

With professionalization come conflicts between what was and what is, and between what is and what (if all goes well) will be. Nurses find their new professional assertiveness coming into conflict with the dominance of medicine and the constraints of hospital employment. The detachment that is one of the earmarks of professional status is set against the involvement that is expected when care and emotional skills are defined as part of the special province of nursing.

As medicine has moved to abandon some of its lower-order diagnostic and treatment tasks, paramedical occupations like physicians' assistants and nurse practitioners have arisen to pick them up. So, in essence, at the same time nursing is attempting to define a special territory, one of its most prestigious specialties, the nurse practitioner, defines its territory as sloughed off medical tasks. This is a third area of conflict in nursing.

These inconsistencies were clearly at the bottom of the controversy surrounding the granting of New Jersey nurses the right to pronounce a person dead. The Board of Medical Examiners in New Jersey passed a rule giving nurses and paramedics the right to pronounce death when a physician isn't available. New Jersey's Board of Nursing opposed the rule on the grounds that it needed time to study the issue, in part to decide whether the ruling should by rights be made by the Board of Nursing (Whitlow, 1982).

Nurses and Death

In a study comparing the attitudes of physicians and nurses toward death, Campbell, Abernethy, and Waterhouse (1983–84) found differences that were tied to professional roles, not to gender, as popular notions would suggest. Their samples consisted of interns and residents, and nurses, at a university medical center. Nurses tended to see a more positive meaning in death than did physicians, that is, as rebirth rather than abandonment, as tranquil rather than frightening. The study assumed that differences in professional roles were the major influence in coloring the definition of "the persistent daily professional contact with death that these individuals experience" (47).

> House officer [physicians'] responses characteristically clustered around the notion of "one who is responsible." Nurses' responses, on the other hand, centered around the central idea of "one who cares." Housestaff repeatedly emphasized their unique position as decision maker and the preemptory component of this part of the physicians' role. In contrast, nurses emphasized their "caring" role from the perspective of performing nursing care procedures as well as providing interpersonal nurturance. (46)

The fact that nurses have less responsibility for diagnostic and treatment decisions "reduces the implication of patient death as professional failure" (48). However, if nursing continues to move along the professionalization track and if, as a result, nurses are given greater responsibility in diagnosis and treatment, then perhaps their attitudes toward death will move closer to those of physicians. As nurses become more susceptible to the strains that physicians experience at a patient's death, it is possible that they will retreat farther behind the shield of professional detachment. This is particularly likely if nursing follows the medical model of professional status.

Ironically, at the same time this is happening in nursing, there is a movement in the opposite direction in medicine, that is, toward more humanized care. This has resulted in part from the assault on the dominant position of medicine (Zola and Miller, 1973) as well as the recent glut of medical services with its resultant competition for patients. This shaking of the ground under medicine was also responsible for the movement toward honesty in telling patients of their impending deaths (MacDougall, 1980). Cynically put, MacDougall suggests that "a doctor who is honest may avoid a malpractice suit" (418).

This tendency toward detachment by nurses will be exacerbated by the structural conditions of their most typical work setting, the hospital. As Jeanne Quint Benoliel (1977:138) observed,

Despite increased attention in nursing education to the psychosocial needs of dying patients and the development of a corps of clinical nursing specialists who have learned to interact constructively with dying patients and their families, the structural conditions of health-care work—especially in hospitals—work against the delivery of personalized services by even the most committed of individuals.

This dysfunction between the ideal culture of professional schools and the real culture of professional work settings is, of course, a dissonant theme running through professional socialization in all the helping professions.

SUMMARY

Some of the treatment of dying patients stems from the fact that occupations in health care are typically professions. This means that they have legitimate control over their own work. This control is granted because an occupation has been able to persuade people with power of the justice of its claims.

Accompanying this process of professionalization is the shift of "dirty work" (often including human-contact tasks) to lower levels in the division of labor. Professional ideologies also support emotional detachment from patients. This reserve becomes one of the traits of the working personality of the professional.

Physicians (and nurses, less so, but increasingly) are committed to cure and not to care. Death is consequently seen as a professional failure. Physicians see death as the enemy to be defeated, which makes the handling of inevitable deaths problematic. In addition, a person's choice of medicine as a career and the choice of specialty within medicine are influenced to an extent by the presence of death as a regular reality of work. There is some suggestion in the literature that people who enter medicine do so in part to overcome their above-average fear of death.

Medical schools include death education as a relatively minor part of the curriculum. With minimal formal training in handling death, physicians' attitudes develop in response to the realities of their medical school and clinical experiences. Coombs and Powers, who proposed a five-stage model to describe the course of this development, acknowledge that reaching the last stage, the transcendence of avoidance and emotional suppression, is hindered by inadequate formal death education and a professional ideology that encourages precisely that avoidance and suppression.

Nursing may follow medicine's path. Although it is currently committed to the emotional as well as the physical care of dying patients, the contradictions inherent in the move toward professionalization may create conditions that encourage nurses to retreat behind professional detachment.

The consequence of this possibility for the treatment of dying patients is clear: an intensification of some of the attitudes and behaviors that make being a patient difficult and that make being a dying patient especially poignant. If these circumstances produce this result, the care of the dying will more than ever be entrusted, borrowing Weber's (1958b:182) phrase, to "specialists without spirit."

Notes

1. In a survey of 1,093 physicians who graduated between 1972 and 1975 from the five medical schools sampled, 20 percent had has an entire course devoted to death, 30 percent had the subject covered in other courses, and 50 percent had no formal death education at all (Dickinson and Pearson, 1980–81). If a significant difference in death attitudes is produced only taking an entire course, then 70 percent of physicians graduating from those medical schools between 1972 and 1975 had no formal death education that influenced their treatment of dying patients. If that represents the figure after the rise of the death education movement, the figure before 1972 is even lower.

It seems safe to say that most physicians have had little, if any, formal death education early in their professional socialization.

2. Although they use the term in relation to organizations, the same effect may be produced by occupations.

CHAPTER SIX
GRIEF AND BEREAVEMENT IN THEIR SOCIAL AND CULTURAL CONTEXT

"Grief," Erich Lindemann (1963:703) wrote, "is the state of pain, discomfort, and often mental and physical impairment that in most persons follows the loss of a loved one [emphasis added]". In other words, it often, but not always, accompanies *bereavement,* the condition of loss and the status that goes with it. Richard Kalish (1981:218) has neatly defined this relationship: "It seems fair to say that you can't grieve without being bereaved, but you can be bereaved and not grieve."

Although grief seems a particularly personal emotion, its onset and course can only be understood in their social and cultural context. This should be kept in mind as you read what follows. When the symptoms of "normal" grief are described, your immediate recognition of them should not cloud the extent to which the meaning of the emotions that comprise grief is rooted in culture.

THE CONFIGURATION OF GRIEF AND THE PROCESS OF GRIEVING

In his study of bereaved hospital patients, relatives of hospital patients who had died, survivors of a Boston nightclub fire, and relatives of members of the armed services, the psychiatrist Erich Lindemann (1944) described the components of a typical grief reaction, what he called, "the symptomatology of normal grief." Lindemann claimed that in all these groups, reactions to bereavement were strikingly similar. The symptoms of normal grief included *bodily distress,* a *preoccupation with the image of the deceased, guilt, hostility,* and *alteration or loss of normal patterns of conduct.* Bodily distress may take the form of exhaustion, loss of appetite, or shortness of breath, for example. The bereaved may picture a scene from memory or may imagine the deceased calling to them or talking to them. Guilt may involve the recitation of events leading up to the death that might have been altered if the bereaved had only tried harder. Warmth may evaporate from relationships with others and be replaced by irritability and unprovoked hostility. Finally, agitation and restlessness replace normally purposive patterns of conduct. In addition, social activities and skills that involved the deceased, such as meeting new people, may be lost.

How long these symptoms persist depends on how successfully the bereaved do their *grief work,* "[the] emancipation from the bondage to the deceased, readjustment to the environment in which the deceased is missing, and the formation of new relationships" (Lindemann, 1944:144). Grief work is painful and difficult, and some people are unwilling or unable to face it. The failure to do grief work may result in morbid, that is, pathological, grief reactions. In pathological grief reactions, the symptoms of normal grief are present, but in wildly exaggerated form. Exhaustion may verge on catatonic paralysis, preoccupation may become a painful, obsessive fixation excluding all other thoughts, guilt may become self-destructive, even suicidal, irritability may become violent rage, and the suspension of social interaction may become permanent and total.

A study by Clayton, Desmarais, and Winokur (1968) of bereavement symptoms, however, found only three symptoms that were experienced by more than half of their subjects, adult relatives of hospital patients who had died: *depressed mood, sleep disturbance,* and *crying. Difficulty concentrating, loss of interst in TV and news,* and *anorexia and/or weight loss* also occurred frequently. However, guilt, hostility, and preoccupation with the image of the deceased were uncommon in the reports of their sample, and bodily distress was rarely as intense as Lindemann described.

The differences between the symptoms found in these two studies may be due in part to differences in the samples. Lindemann studied people he met in the course of his clinical practice. Clayton, Desmarais, and Winokur's work was "an attempt to study the symptoms of bereavement in a group of people who were selected by means other than consulting a physician and therefore may represent a normal reaction to bereavement" (64). Considering the suddeness and horror with which the Boston nightclub victims died, it is understandable that their survivors might be preoccupied with the image of the deceased or feel guilt at surviving while those they loved had died.

The components of grieving seem to include all of the symptoms mentioned in the two studies, although their strength and distribution vary considerably by group and by culture. Guilt, for example, was present in from 0 percent to 79 percent of the bereaved subjects of twelve studies summarized by Miles and Demi (1983–84), being lowest for Japanese widows and highest for bereaved psychiatric patients.

Bereavement and the grief work it often entails play themselves out over time. Several models of their course have been advanced.

Geoffrey Gorer (1965:29) in his study of grief and mourning in Great Britain suggests that three stages constitute the "normal" pattern of "time-limited mourning,"[1] although he acknowledges that this is only one pattern among many. It was in fact followed by only twenty-five of the eighty people he interviewed in depth. These stages are (1) *shock,* usually lasting until the funeral is over; (2) *intense mourning,* involving emotional withdrawal and bodily distress, and lasting roughly six to twelve weeks; and (3) a *restoration* of a relatively normal social and emotional condition.

Kathy Charmaz (1980:298–307) focuses on the changes in self-image that grieving often involves. She also acknowledges that grief may take many courses. However, she explains that the major ones in American society are *transition, realization,* and *reintegration.* In transition, the bereaved feels the acute distress of a life disrupted and sees the world with a certain sense of unreality. This is produced in part by the tendency of family and friends to take over the tasks the bereaved might otherwise have to handle. Whatever the motives, the underlying message is that the bereaved is incapable of handling anything. In the stage of realization, the bereaved, no longer surrounded by supportive mourners, is left alone to deal with the loss of the deceased and also the loss of that part of the self that was bound up with the deceased. As one reaction, the bereaved may identify more strongly with the deceased, who becomes, in Charmaz's words, "a symbolic source of reference" (303). In that way the bereaved may become more like the deceased, both to commemorate and to hang on. Realization gives way to reintegration in which ongoing identification with the deceased may provide a sense of continuity to balance the redirection and new interests that develop. This stage involves not merely a return to social life, but "a *reorganization* of the subjective self " (307) into a postgrief-work self.

Hardt (1978–79:283–284) attempts to ground a sequence of five stages of grief and mourning (which he calls "stages of bereavement") in time as Table 6-1 illustrates. These models of grief and grieving must be situated in terms of culture and historical period as well as social and economic factors. Each of the three discussed does this to an extent.

Gorer (1965:ix) limits his findings to Great Britain, although he expresses the belief that "the main theme of the book, the social denial and the individual repudiation of mourning," applies as well to the majority of Americans. Charmaz confines her model to major patterns in the United States. There are also implicit limitations in generalizing the results of Hardt's study. Taken together, it is clear that grief fol-

TABLE 6-1   Stages of Grief

Stages	Duration	Major Emotional Themes
I	From time of death up to one month	Denial
II	From one up to two months	False acceptance
III	From two up to three months	Pseudoreorganization
IV	From three up to eight months	Depression
V	Eight months and longer	Reorganization/acceptance

Source: Hardt (1978–79:283–284).

lows patterns although the room for individual variation is considerable.

Culture and Grief

Culture affects grief in a number of ways.[2] Culture influences what sort of loss a death will involve. In some cultures, traditional Chinese, for example, the deceased has a chance to move up in the afterworld and consequently to gain by death. Social valuation of the dying, which was discussed in detail in Chapter Three, also influences the degree of loss that will be felt. Fulton and Fulton (1971) describe this range by saying that some deaths have high grief potential and others low grief potential. They do not equate low grief potential with *no* grief potential; that is, some grief may be felt at the death of an elderly relative. Low grief potential simply suggests less likelihood of a profound grief experience.

Culture also affects whose loss a death will be. In matrilineal cultures, you are related to your mother's kin. Consequently, the death of a member of your father's family, or your biological father himself, for that matter, is not your loss. To mourn that death would be inappropriate. An informal equation exists to rank the degree of loss attached to a death. Since in American society we are expected to express grief on the death of those close to us, this same equation serves as a prescription for grief. At one end would be the death of someone in our immediate family, that is, a high-grief-*expectation* death. At the other end would be the death of someone to whom we have no close formal relationship, but with whom we may have a deep emotional involvement nonetheless, that is, a low-grief-*expectation* death. These deaths might include people for whom intense mourning would be considered nonlegitimate (e.g., teachers or co-workers) and people for whom intense mourning would be considered illegitmate, that is, gay lovers or mistresses. Fudin and Devore (n.d.) call these survivors "the unidentified bereaved," people who feel grief, but have no acceptable right to mourn.

Perhaps at the bottom of the scale would be the death of pets (see Chapter Ten). If it's difficult to imagine being granted an exemption from normal responsibilities to mourn the death of a friend, it's almost inconceivable to be granted that exemption to mourn the death of a pet.

Although the calculus is usually informal, it is sometimes formalized. One example is the stipulations in contracts covering allowable paid absences for deaths. The contract between the New York City Board of Education (1984) and the United Federation of Teachers grants four days with pay for a death in the immediate family. The membership in the "immediate family" is specified as "a parent, child, brother, sister, grandparent, grandchild, husband, wife, or parent of a husband or wife, or any relative residing in the employee's household."

Culture also affects the opportunity to express grief. British culture, Gorer (1965:133) points out, allows no outlet for the destructive impulses that bereavement often generates. Other cultures do, for example, by requiring the ritual destruction of the deceased's possessions. Gorer suggests that this unspent anger may be turned inward as self-punishment or guilt or outward as wanton destructiveness.

A consequence of this denial of mourning, Gorer claims, is a fixation on death expressed as either repulsion by death or attraction to violence.

> The constant complaints about the depiction of "violence" on television or cinema screen are as symptomatic as the preoccupation with death and cruelty in the "horror films" and "horror comics" and the endless spate of ill-written paperback books on the horrors of war and concentration camps. The "pornography of death," whether it be furtively enjoyed or self-righteously condemned, manifests an irrational attitude towards death and a denial of mourning. (132)

Culture affects the manner in which grief is expressed. Because of the constraints of the Protestant Ethos (discussed in Chapter Three), grief becomes "a *private* affair" (Charmaz, 1980:285). Charmaz claims that Americans feel uncomfortable about displaying any strong feelings, grief among them, in front of others. Yet, on the other hand, people are expected to cry.

This expectation must also be reconciled with those attached to other roles. Although less true than it once was, men are still expected not to cry in front of others, while women are expected to do precisely the opposite. (Volkart and Michael, 1957:298–299).

Another aspect of social structure, family structure, also leaves its imprint on grieving. Volkart and Michael (292–295) argue that in cultures where children are brought up in extended families, the death of any one member of the family has less impact than does the death of one of two parents in nuclear family systems. In a nuclear family, parents become the repositories of both love and hate, so that the bereaved have to deal with their grief and their hostility, and their consequent guilt, all at the same time.

A final example of the intersection of cultural expectations and grief is the increasing importance of anticipatory grief and its consequences. Anticipatory grief is grief work completed in anticipation of death. Fulton and Fulton (1971) argue that anticipatory grief is becoming increasingly prevalent. The elderly are often isolated in nursing homes and retirement communities, and the family's grief work often begins at the time of separation. The family adjusts to the world in which the elderly relative no longer plays a part. By the time the death actually occurs months or years later, it is an anticlimax.

The prolongation of dying creates another circumstance that encourages anticipatory grieving. If a person is hospitalized and dies over a long period of time, the family is forced to adjust to home life without the patient. Emotional energy may also be dissipated in frequent hospital visits and the daily crises of the patient's terminal illness.

Anticipatory grief has several consequences. While bereavement after the actual death may pass more smoothly, it may also be made more difficult by the guilt that comes from feeling nothing in a situation that demands intense feeling. Another possible consequence is the streamlining of funeral rituals because the bereaved need little help in reorienting themselves to the world. The other functions of funerals, such as promoting a sense of group identification, are lost in the bargain. Finally, the dying must cope not only with impending death, but with the seeming indifference of their relatives (Fulton and Fulton, 1971).

GRIEF WITHOUT DEATH: GRIEF AND BEREAVEMENT IN QUASI-DEATH EXPERIENCES[3]

Anticipatory grief involves either grief at impending death or grief at social death (to use Sudnow's term in an expanded sense). Social death may be precipitated, for example, by the separation involved in an elderly relative moving to a distant retirement community. In other words, for an experience to precipitate the reactions that ordinarily accompany mourning a death, it must resemble death in important respects. It must involve some combination of *separation, termination,* and *loss.* These experiences that resemble death are called *quasi-death experiences.* It's tempting to say that experiences like divorce, broken friendships, retirement, being fired, moving out of a community, and graduation[4] aren't necessarily permanent, whereas real death means an absolute separation from the deceased. After all, you can always visit your old neighborhood or run into your former spouse. But, the distinction isn't that clear-cut. If you believe in an afterlife, then real death is hardly permanent. On the other hand, you can visit your old place of employment, but nothing's to say that it will not have changed beyond recognition in the interim. You can visit your old house, but, as Thomas Wolfe recognized, you can't go home again.

Just as grief may or may not accompany bereavement in real-death situations, the same is true in quasi-death experiences. When grief does occur in quasi-death, it tends to have the same configuration and follow the same course as in real death. You only have to point to the preoccupation with the image of the "deceased" after romantic break-ups to understand this point.

Both experiences also may involve crucial changes in identity. Grief work in both cases involves an adjustment to a world in which this person (as in divorce) or this sense of yourself (as in the loss of a job) no longer has a part. The adjustment entails a reconstruction of your sense of self. Just as we sometimes can only be a certain way with one other person, the same is true of occupational careers. In both cases, when the person dies or the job is done, that version of ourselves often ends with it.

Retirement is a good example of this quality of quasi-death experiences. Retirement means the end of work. In a culture where the Protestant ethos is so strong and virtually the only dignity people have comes from their work, the end of work often means the end of dignity. Retirement also means the likely end of contact with an important reference group, other workers (Blau, 1956). It also may mean the end of a certain life-style and, as a rite of passage, the end of middle age. To say that these endings would likely have a significant effect on a person's self would border on understatement.

The only clear-cut difference between the two types of experiences is the fact that in quasi-death you can't count on as much social and ritual support. Because people don't usually recognize the similarity of quasi-death to real death, you can't usually count on as much support from friends, family, and employers in quasi-death experiences. In addition, few ritual supports exist to prop up the "bereaved." Graduation and the recent advent of "divorce parties" may seem exceptions. But mourning is hardly allowed in the festive atmosphere of these events.

The ending of one phase of a role career or self is at the heart of the quasi-death experience. Social forces form the context in which these changes take place, because they influence a person's movement through these careers. Factors that influence a person's movement through a role career are called *career contingencies* (Goffman, 1961:134–135). Contingencies influencing quasi-death experiences include the degree of social and geographical mobility in a society, the pace of social and economic change, and the divorce rate. The proportion of quasi-deaths to real deaths would also rise in a society where the death rate is low and where death is concentrated in one age group, for example, the elderly. Young people in American society, in which all of these factors operate, have relatively few real death experiences but many quasi-death experiences.

SUMMARY

The emotions of grief and the state of bereavement must be seen in their social and cultural context. Models of the configuration of normal grief vary to some extent, but there is a core of symptoms that seems to be common to most grief in America. The variations in lists of symptoms seem to be a function of the groups studied. The same is true for models of the course that grief follows.

Where grief is present, grief work seems a necessary task for the bereaved. Again, different societies provide greater or lesser opportunities to do grief work.

Culture defines the appropriate occasion for grief, and the manner in which grief is expressed. It also influences the content of grief. Elements of social structure such as sex roles and family structure also affect grief and the course of grieving.

Changes in society have increased the importance of anticipatory grief. These changes also affect grief in quasi-death experiences.

Sociology attempts to study grief to describe it, explain it in terms of sociological variables, and use these explanations to predict its course. The understanding derived from that study also, though indirectly, has a practical consequence, to make us receptive to the power of grief in ourselves and in others, in death experiences and in experiences that resemble death. If it is possible to underestimate its effects in ourselves, it is even easier to underestimate it in others. As Shakespeare wrote, "Every one can master a grief but he that has it."

Notes

1. Gorer uses mourning to include both the emotional state and the behavior that often accompany bereavement. Mourning, in the sense of that behavior alone, will be discussed in Chapter Seven.

2. This discussion relies heavily on Volkart and Michael (1957).

3. The idea of quasi-death experiences was suggested by Lindemann (1944). The term is my own (Kamerman, 1985).

4. An interesting example of a quasi-death experience is finishing a college or graduate degree. Perhaps one reason people avoid endings is their inability to face the loss of that part of their lives. The qualifying degree in academic disciplines is, appropriately enough, called the "terminal degree."

CHAPTER SEVEN
MOURNING: PUBLIC AND PRIVATE

Robert Blauner (1966) maintains that the place of the dead in a society, that is, the extent to which death disrupts the functioning of that society, and the funerary rituals that reflect that place, are good mirrors of the social structure and values of that society. In this chapter, the mourning rituals of American society will be examined as much to understand American values and social structure as to understand death and mourning.

These societal reflections are found in public as well as private mourning. Public here means not simply behavior in front of the family and the community, for example, funerals and memorial services, but also the mourning for public figures, presidents, personalities, and prophets. Private mourning, the more personal, less publicly accessible behavior of bereavement, must also be situated in its cultural and historical context to be understood. Changes in the public funeral influence the course and character of private mourning. As values and social structure change, mourning changes with them.

PUBLIC MOURNING: FUNERALS

The Functions of Funerals

Funerals perform a number of important functions. David Mandelbaum (1959:195–198), in a study of Kota society in Southern India, mentions several. The most obvious is the removal of the body. In addition, the ceremony guides the bereaved through their grief back to the world of the living. The rituals are a public acknowledgment by the group of the loss of one of its members. At the same time, these rituals reaffirm the survival of the social structure beyond the loss of one member. In funeral homes people sit by rank, the immediate family closest to the casket, other family members behind them, then friends, business associates, and neighbors. This is a diagram of the group memberships of the deceased in order of socially acknowledged importance. It symbolizes the fact that a family member is dead, but the family survives; a friend is dead, but the friendship group survives; and so on. Similarly, Kota ceremonies symbolize the survival of both structure and rank.

Funerals also provide an opportunity to do grief work, or at the very least, a legitimate occasion to express grief. The expression of grief, like the expression of other emotions, is contained by the prescriptions of culture. Culture defines the proper amount of grief. Too much, for example, throwing yourself on the casket in a funeral home, and family rushes forward to douse your grief. Too little, and people infer that no grief is felt (although in American culture, where the display of any strong emotion is suspect, little display of grief is often interpreted as courage and strength).

Funerals also allow people to pay tribute to the dead, both verbally and monetarily. This literal tribute, funeral expenditures, functions to demonstrate feelings of loss to others and also to expiate possible guilt felt about the deceased. In fact, unlike gifts given to children in place of attention, funeral expenditures represent for many the only opportunity left to settle up with the dead.

Much controversy has surrounded funeral expenditures. Jessica Mitford, in her 1963 book *The American Way of Death*, sees the money spent on funerals as the result of the wiles of funeral directors who prey on the bereaved in their most vulnerable moment. Mitford (22–38) points out that the buyer of funeral services is unlike other consumers in several respects. Funeral consumers are emotionally agitated, wonder what the proper thing to do is, are almost totally ignorant of what to expect at the funeral home, and must make quick decisions as they do not have time to comparison shop. They are generally ignorant of the law, relying on the funeral director's knowledge. Finally, the bereaved sometimes have a chunk of cash, insurance and death benefits, to spend. Funeral directors have a finite market: people die only once. The best way to increase their income is to expand the range of services they sell on each occasion. Mitford sums up her position at the outset:

> O Death, where is thy sting? O grave, where is thy victory? Where, indeed. Many a badly stung survivor, faced with the aftermath of some relative's funeral, has ruefully concluded that the victory has been won hands down by a funeral establishment—in a disastrously unequal battle. (15)

The Consumer Union (1977) takes a more balanced, but ultimately similar, position, arguing that although funeral homes are businesses and profits are to be expected, those profits are unjustifiably high. Some funeral directors fail to inform their customers about the costs of goods, services, and less expensive alternatives in a way that would allow those customers to make intelligent decisions.

In addition, the Consumer Union points to some funeral directors who actively take advantage of the bereaved. In sum, the funeral industry as a whole is guilty, according to the Consumer Union of sins of omission and commission, respectively. It is, of course, interesting that an ethical standard is applied to the funeral industry, for example, informing customers of less costly alternatives, that the Consumer Union would not apply to other businesses. The paradoxical position of the funeral director as entrepreneur, professional, and secular substitute for family and priest in the handling of the dead is at the base of this demand.

A very different view of funeral expenditures is taken by Vanderlyn Pine and Derek Phillips (1970). Taking specific issue with Mitford's position (416), they see funeral expenditures as the secular equivalent of the religious practices surrounding death that have slipped in importance.

> Our view is that *because* people increasingly lack both the ceremonial and social mechanisms that once existed to help them cope with death, monetary expenditures have taken on added importance as a means for allowing the bereaved to express (both to themselves and others) their sentiments for the deceased. For with so few modes of expression remaining to the bereaved, funeral expenditures serve as evidence of their concern for both the dead and the conventional standards of decency in their community of residence. (416)

If funeral expenditures are a barometer of concern for the dead, then the resentment against them is perhaps a reflection of the diminishing place of the dead in American society (Blauner, 1966). Funerals that used to be community affairs are now conducted by and for family and friends. The death of any one individual, with the possible exception of a public figure, fails to be noticed, let alone to disrupt the functioning of modern mass societies. In essence, any given individual is irrelevant to the functioning of society. It is because of this that funerals have become an individual family's concern. The funeral, Blauner claims, is losing its significance.

Changes in the Form and Functions of Funerals

At the same time that a death has become less socially disruptive, it has become more personally traumatic. A person in contemporary society is bereaved less often than people in past or simpler societies. In addition, Blauner maintains, mourning has become less a communal event than a private crisis. We face bereavement unprepared by experience, alone, and without the comfort of beliefs in something larger than ourselves. Funeral rituals, which have their origins in a time when people were on familiar terms with death, when people faced bereavement in the midst of their community, and when beliefs were held that found expression in isomorphic rituals often seem artificial and absurd. If the best alternative is to follow a ritual in which you believe, perhaps the worst is to feel forced to follow a ritual you no longer believe in.

In effect, rituals no longer provide the support they once did. As Robert Fulton (1976:342) succinctly put it,

Simply stated, the meaning of a prayer today is lost upon a person who holds no religious beliefs. So, too, a ceremony that invites all to mourn a death presents serious difficulties for the person who has come to believe his grief is private and personal.

This *deritualization of mourning* (Fulton, 1965:335) reflects not only changes in the meaning of death, but also much stronger currents in American society. Deritualization strains against the past in American culture in general. America's future orientation makes the confrontation with history, both personal and national, a difficult task. The shifting of national holidays to Mondays to make three-day weekends and provide occasions for store sales symbolizes the ascendance of leisure and commercialism over tradition. When a society takes its first president's birthday and moves it to a Monday, it changes the meaning of George Washington from the father of his country to the emblem of the Washington's Birthday Sale.

David Mandelbaum (1959:214–215) also holds that American culture has become deritualized, but feels that new rituals will arise to replace the ones that were lost. He claims that the functions of these rituals will be the same as what went before although their content may change. However, the succession of rituals is not always smoothly accomplished. There are usually periods during which old rituals are questioned and no new rituals have yet become acceptable substitutes. What Orrin Klapp (1969:viii) wrote about symbols is as true of rituals: "The unfortunate thing about symbols is that they are not replaced as easily as tires, rebuilt as easily as houses, or easily manufactured; often they are better when older."

The growth of memorial societies is further evidence of this deritualization. Memorial societies are organizations whose purpose is to educate consumers of funeral services about the costs involved in funerals, alternatives to traditional funerals, legal requirements for body disposal, and so on. They also represent a lobby for the legislative interests of funeral consumers. The goal of these efforts is to enable the bereaved to secure simple, dignified funerals, memorial services, and burials. The first memorial society in the United States was founded in 1939. There were only seven societies in 1959 (Consumer Union, 1977:212). In the 1960s and 1970s, the movement grew rapidly, and by 1983, there were about 175 societies in the United States representing a membership of about 500,000 (Continental Association of Funeral and Memorial Societies, 1983). Memorial societies have several forms, but most often have either a contract or informal arrangement with a local funeral director to provide these "no-frills funerals."

The growth of memorial societies must be seen in two ways. They represent a change in the direction of deritualization and a dissatisfaction with funeral directors and traditional funerals. However, in an absolute sense, they represent a minority both in number and view. Most people seem satisfied with funeral directors and funeral services (Kalish and Goldberg, 1979–80; Doka, 1984–85). That doesn't change the fact that a discernible minority are dissatisfied and that their number is growing.

A second major trend in funeral practices is *rationalization*. Rationalization, in Weber's (1985a:51) usage, means bringing things under control by making them subject to rules, that is, calculable and consequently predictable. Weber felt that what began in the bureaucracies of people's work lives would eventually spill over into their private lives.

A good example of rationalization is the practice of holding "funerals" in the funeral home, an innovation of a Los Angeles funeral director. Because Los Angeles is spread out with a number of population centers connected by freeways, funeral processions originating in one center and ending up at a cemetery on the outskirts of another some distance away are traffic nightmares. A more efficient "funeral" is held at the funeral home: the casket bathed in light, the family around it, the eulogy spoken, the casket lowered into the darkness, tears shed, and the family departing. Once in the basement, caskets can be stacked and driven, singly or in multiples, out to the appropriate cemeteries according to the work schedules of those cemeteries. Deaths and the accompanying cemetery work, formerly unpredictable, can now be brought under rational control. *When* a person dies is no longer the guiding factor; what begins to take its place is the more predictable business consideration of when the cemetery can most efficiently handle the burial.

An even more pointed example of creeping rationalization is found in Lois Pratt's (1981) study of the influence of business temporal norms on mourning. Business translates bereavement into monetary terms. Employment contracts often specify the number of paid leave days granted for bereavement. They also define who is bereaved by stipulating whose deaths constitute grounds for paid leave. In effect, they limit mourners (at least those who would be eligible to mourn without financial sacrifice) to members of the immediate family; that is, they exclude friends.

The trend toward shorter mourning times is reinforced by squeezing the public expression of bereavement into a three-day period. In addition, by limiting "death work" (the preparation and conduct of mourning) to the nuclear family, "we might expect a trend away from elaborate public ritual and toward simplified private rites" (328).

Finally, mourning is homogenized for all members of the family by stipulating the same three days for the deaths of husband, wife, brother, and sister. Business dress codes also supersede mourning dress codes, with the result that all displays of mourning, together with the differences in relationship that they reflect, are done away with.

In sum, funerals are "brief, simple, and private," and mourning in general is brief and uniform for all members of the immediate family (330). An ultimate consequence of rationalized mourning is to promote a certain view of society. Pratt concludes,

> As bereavement practices have been patterned increasingly according to business temporal norms, taking on the shape and meaning of the business system, bereavement has come to reflect and reinforce a view of the social order as efficient, under control, and based on businesslike management of time.

By imposing business temporal norms on bereavement, this formerly erratic process becomes quantifiable and controllable.

A development that has elements of both deritualization and rationalization is the move toward cremation rather than burial for the disposal of the body. Cremation is more common in other countries than in the United States. In Japan, for example, 91.1 percent of those who died in 1980 were cremated, with the percentage in the major cities nearly 100 (Fujii, 1983:47). In the United States, the proportion of cremations was 7 percent in 1976 (Consumer Union, 1977:156), but had risen to about 12.5 percent by 1985 (Krauss, 1985). Among the "advantages" of cremation mentioned by Leroy Bowman (1959:167) are "sanitary benefits and economy of space," emotional comfort to the family, who don't have to contend with "the horrors of slow decay," and a reduction in cost. The Consumer Union (1977:158) pointed to reasons for the trend toward cremation, including a scarcity of cemetery space; methods that are "clean, quick, and efficient"; and, again, lower cost.

The reduction in cost is neutralized to an extent by the provision of funeral services in some cases and the sale of additional services specific to cremation in others. Cremation still entails the disposal of remains, although the problem is simpler. One California enterprise offers cremation and scattering at sea as a package. For an additional fee, a memorial party, complete with food and music on the society's yacht, can also be had (Mitford, 1980:52). Still another network of funeral homes offers to launch cremated remains into earth orbit. Although the first launch hasn't taken place, several hundred reservations have already been made (Krauss, 1985).

As to whether societal changes and the advent of new funerary and memorial practices will perform the functions of the rituals they replace, the answer is not clear. Certainly, the performance of some will be made more difficult. Greater geographical mobility may make it difficult to attend a funeral in the first place and to return to a grave-site for a visitation. But, cremation and scattering make it impossible. The disappearance of older rituals and the ensuing (if perhaps tempo-rary) normative vacuum it creates mean that people don't know the proper thing to do. Until faith is built up in the newer, streamlined rituals, the bereaved may have no way of settling up with the dead. The importance of funeral expenditures to settle debts with the de-ceased (Pine and Phillips, 1970) is a good indication of the absence of other means of paying proper tribute. It is in the crevices between ritu-als and between beliefs that traditional functions are sometimes lost.

While it is possible that the functions of traditional funerals will be performed as well by newer rituals once they become established, Fulton and Fulton (1971) suggest a second possibility. Because death is increasingly the property of the elderly and because the elderly are sometimes segregated out in hospitals, nursing homes, old age homes, and retirement communities, it is possible that by the time they die, their actual deaths are anticlimactic. Anticipatory grief, begun by rel-atives when the elderly enter that segregation, may make grief work easier or perhaps superfluous. As Fulton and Fulton point out, it also has the consequence of making the funeral, one of whose functions is to enable people to do their grief work, seem less necessary. With the loss of one function and the diminished importance of the funeral, other functions may also be lost. As the Fultons observe,

> It [the funeral], like other rituals, ceremonies, rites of passage, pageants and festivals, serves to reinforce a sense of community as it fashions and re-fashions social bonds. The tendency for some family members to mod-ify traditional funeral rites, where no one except the immediate mem-bers of the family are present, or to modify mortuary rites, to the barest requirements, can well be dysfunctional for an extended group of family members, friends, and other survivors. (52)

So, the loss of community that brought about changes in the funeral is in turn reinforced by these changes much as the spread of business temporal norms to bereavement reinforced a sense of society operating in an orderly, businesslike way.

The loss of community doesn't necessarily mean a loss in the need for a sense of community, that is, an identification with something larger than oneself. This is clearly seen in the scale of the outpourings on the deaths of public figures.

Mourning for Public Figures

Public figures are symbols of specific values and beliefs in a soci-ety. As these values and beliefs change, heroes change along with them. The qualities admired in heroes a century ago may no longer be the qualities we admire in heroes today. A 1985 survey (McBee, 1985) found few religious and political leaders numbered among the heroes of the young. Popular culture stars had taken their place. Even the question of whether or not people have heroes is tied to social change. In the 1960s and 1970s, having heroes became unpopular (McBee, 1985:48). With the 1980s, the hero returned. Through all these changes, however, the hero remains a *collective representation* (Durkheim, 1961), a symbol of the values and a reflection of the social structure of a society.

When a leader dies, particularly if the death was unexpected, the survival of the group itself is threatened. Its members feel personally threatened because a leader is each member writ large. Because of this, it becomes important to reassert the viability of the group, both for the group's sake and for each member's sake. In part, this is accomplished by deifying these figures even further: "the deaths of such men also become powerful sacred symbols which organize, direct, and constantly revive the collective ideals of the community and the nation" (Warner, 1962:34). When we pay homage to these dead, we pay homage to our belief in the ideals they represent.

When President John F. Kennedy was assassinated in 1963, many Americans saw his death as their personal loss (Sheatsley and Feldman, 1964). People also expressed feelings of loss as Americans, one of the infrequent occasions when national identity is strongly felt. The next president, Lyndon B. Johnson, was sworn in aboard a plane on his way to Washington, D.C. The necessity to symbolize continuous leadership was very important. This need for continuity is expressed in the salute, "The King is dead. Long live the King!" (Mandelbaum, 1959:213).

In addition to restoring a sense of continuity, funerals and other memorial rites for public figures function to promote a sense of grouphood. W. Lloyd Warner's (1962) analysis of Memorial Day illustrates both these functions. Memorial Day is a symbol of unity in the face of the diverse groups and diverse interests in American life. It is also a transcendence of death, because a person can confront fears "with a system of sacred beliefs about death" (8). The ceremonies allow people to relive a time when national unity was at its strongest, a time of war (28).

Cemeteries that honor the war dead are tangible opportunities to tap the glory of the past. Cemeteries are the interface of life and death. "The symbols of death," Warner concludes, "say what life is and those of life define what death must be" (19). The national cemetery system and the Tomb of the Unknowns in Arlington National Cemetery in particular are monuments to the importance attached to the dead as collective representations of sacrifice, loyalty, and honor. The tomb, with its moving inscription, "Here rests in honored glory an American soldier known but to God," exemplifies the need to preserve in a permanent and visible way the memory of war dead and the values and unity they represent. The annual celebration of Memorial Day demonstrates the needs to relive these memories over and over again.

In 1986, the American space shuttle *Challenger* exploded shortly after lift-off, killing all seven astronauts aboard. The families of those astronauts had been invited to Cape Canaveral to watch the launch. A New Hampshire high school teacher had been selected to ride aboard the shuttle, and her students watched on television as the shuttle exploded.

What was a terrible personal tragedy for those families and students was transformed into a national tragedy and a test of faith in technology in general and the space program in particular. It also became the occasion for national mourning. The astronauts became, in Warner's words, "powerful symbols" of faith in the correctness of the government's space research, the courage of pioneers, and the virtue of science and technology. The crew also represented several American ideals. A teacher included among professional astronauts was a symbol of the greatness of "ordinary" people. There were also in the crew both men and women, a Japanese American, and a black American. Although in a number of senses they were extraordinary people, their ordinariness was stressed in the media.

Memorial ceremonies were held and tributes made for days afterwards. Condolences from leaders around the world were sent to the United States. Flags were flown at half staff. Bells throughout Houston, site of the Johnson Space Center, tolled for 7 minutes. A memorial service led by President Ronald Reagan was held at the Johnson Space Center. During the service, jets flew overhead in a memorial formation in which one plane is missing. President Reagan eulogized the dead as individuals, but emphasized the desire of their families to have the shuttle program continue. A wreath of flowers was dropped into the waters off Cape Canaveral. The Soviet Union named two craters on Venus for the two women crew members.

These events also became the occasion for public discussion of how to handle the shock and grief of the children across the country who had watched the launch on television. Finally, speeches and eulogies emphasized over and over that space exploration must continue as a tribute to the seven who died.

The funerals of public figures provide an opportunity to study a society's views of death and the dead. The actor Rudolph Valentino's death in 1926 resulted in riots around the funeral home in New York. For publicity, actresses were hired to wail outside the funeral home, which precipitated the riot. Those inside feared that the casket, the body, the flowers, and the home itself might be ripped apart by the crowd anxious to carry off some shred to preserve the memory of their fallen idol.

If the public is denied the opportunity to express its grief and ceremonially acknowledge its hero, the pent-up necessity remains. The opera composer and national hero Giuseppe Verdi, for example, left instructions that his funeral be simple. In accordance with his wishes, the funeral procession was small and modest. One month later, when his body was reburied in a crypt at the home he had established for retired musicians, 200,000 people (accompanied by a 900-member chorus) attended the ceremony. As Francis Toye (1946:194) wrote,

> This event evoked an extraordinary demonstration on the part of the citizens of Milan, who felt that, whereas the first funeral had rightly been celebrated in accordance with the wishes of the composer, they were now justified in seizing upon the reinterment as an opportunity to show their own feelings.

Perhaps the most touching tribute to a public figure was accorded posthumously to the ballet dancer Anna Pavlova. At her company's first performance after her death, the orchestra played the music to her most famous dance, "The Dying Swan," in a darkened theater in Brussels as a spotlight moved around the stage following where she would have been. The audience stood and wept.

The formation of cults around dead heroes, for example, the actor James Dean, the singer Elvis Presley, the magician Harry Houdini, involves the inability to accept the finality of death. In Houdini's case, groups gather at his grave on the anniversary of his death waiting for a sign from beyond. The bumper sticker sold after Elvis Presley's death clearly articulates this hope for immortality: "Elvis [Presley] didn't die. He just moved on to a better town."

There is another function that mourning for public figures performs. These occasions provide a legitimate, sometimes even patriotic, opportunity to express displaced grief and may serve as a trigger for delayed grief. One study of schizophrenics in a therapy group found that President Kennedy's death became the occasion to express the group's grief over the death of a former group leader (Dumont, 1966, cited in Vernon, 1970:150). As the ritual opportunities to do grief work in personal bereavements diminish, or in periods of change between the disappearance of old and the development of new rituals, the ceremonies surrounding the deaths of public figures become even more important opportunities to unload grief.

PRIVATE MOURNING: GORER'S STYLES OF MOURNING

The distinction between public and private mourning is difficult to draw clearly. As suggested earlier, private mourning is colored by the standards of our culture and our times. But when the funeral is over, we are alone, and often drag our grief around for years afterward.

The English anthropologist Geoffrey Gorer (1965) studied patterns of mourning, arranging them on the basis of the length of mourning. He delineated eight "styles of mourning." The first, *denial of mourning,* is often rooted in religious beliefs that denied the finality of death. One woman, who believed in reincarnation, merely visited the cemetery where her family was buried to see if a headstone had been properly put up. Otherwise, she engaged in no public mourning.

A similar style, *absence of mourning,* is based not on religious beliefs but on the absence of emotional ties to the deceased. This may be related to another style, *mourning before death,* which is similar to anticipatory grief that, as Fulton and Fulton (1971) point out, increasingly accompanies, in some contemporary societies, the prolongation of life by modern medicine and the isolation and irrelevance of the elderly.

Hiding grief involves the bereaved's attempting "to 'carry on,' to 'keep busy,' to act, at least in public, as if nothing had happened" (71–72). While Gorer sees this as a personal response to bereavement, it is clear that this sort of response is encouraged by the imposition of business temporal norms on mourning. By the same token, mourning is constrained by economic and social factors. If you need to go back to work or back to school or in other ways resume your public life, hiding grief becomes a necessity.

The most common pattern, *time-limited mourning,* involves a period of intense grief followed by a gradual return to normal activities. Gorer included in this group mourners who followed prescribed rituals and those who went through a similar sequence although they followed no prescribed rituals. Just as people are expected to display some grief, but not "too much," people are expected to mourn for a period of time, but not for "too long."

At the other extreme is a category called *unlimited mourning: "never get over,"* in which mourners claimed to feel an ongoing grief although it didn't seem to disrupt the conduct of their lives. In *unlimited mourning: mummification,* a room or a house was left exactly as it was when the deceased died. This style is somewhat disruptive. If the objects with which we surround ourselves are symbols of identities we try to communicate to others, the preservation of a scene as it was when the deceased was alive is an attempt to freeze that part of ourselves; to that extent, it disrupts the change that is normal in our lives.[1]

In the final style, *unlimited mourning: despair,* mourning is accompanied by deep emotional pain. Gorer saw a relationship between this pattern and the availability of rituals to steer people through their grief.

> The number of people in despair—9 out of 80—was a surprise to me. I am inclined to see a connection between this inability to get over grief and the absence of any ritual either individual or social, lay or religious, to guide them and the people they come in contact with. (91)

The styles of mourning Gorer delineated fall into three categories: little or no mourning, time-limited mourning, and unlimited mourning. If they are characterized by their social meanings, they become too little, just right, and too much. These social judgments constitute the measure of mourning both to others and to the bereaved.

SUMMARY

This chapter examined the behavior, both public and private, that accompanies bereavement. Public mourning was defined as both funerary and memorial behavior in front of family and community, and mourning for public figures.

Funerals were examined first to understand their functions and then to see how these functions are performed as funerals change. Funerals dispose of the body, symbolize the social web in which the deceased's life was lived, and reaffirm the survival of that social structure beyond the loss of one of its members. Funerals also provide an opportunity to do grief work.

Funerals have come under attack as the expensive, unnecessary residue of an ignorant past. Critics see the funeral as being unlike other consumer transactions in the sense that the customer is in an unusually vulnerable position. But, more significant, they see it at base as a consumer transaction. An alternate view of funeral expenditures was presented. In the view of Pine and Phillips, the context of disappearing rituals to guide the bereaved, funeral expenditures may be one of the few means left in contemporary society to pay proper tribute to the dead.

The two major trends in public mourning have been deritualization and rationalization. Deritualization reflects the increasing irrelevance of the dead in contemporary society, that is, the death of no one person disrupts the smooth functioning of society as it does in small village societies. Deritualization in mourning also reflects deritualization in American society in general. The shifting of holidays for purposes of commerce and leisure reflects this trend. The growth of memorial societies dedicated to promoting "no-frills funerals" is also an evidence of deritualization. Rationalization of mourning is evidenced by the imposition of business time norms on bereavement. They attempt to make bereavement manageable by redefining it as a business problem calculable in monetary terms. The growing popularity of cremation involves both deritualization and rationalization.

Whether these newer practices will perform the functions of more traditional funerary and memorial rituals is still open to question. It does seem likely that in the period before these newer practices become traditions themselves, a period we are in today, the bereaved will be left with little normative support.

The mourning for public figures represents a pocket of tradition in the general welter of change. Heroes as collective representations embody the values and beliefs of a group. Their deaths threaten the group itself. The mourning rituals for public figures function to sustain a sense of continuity and promote a feeling of grouphood. Heroes and the values and beliefs they embody may change, but their function and the functions of mourning their loss remain the same.

Mourning for public figures also provides an opportunity to unload unspent grief. In a society that provides fewer mechanisms to express grief over the deaths of people in our personal lives, these substitute outlets become increasingly important.

Private mourning was examined by summarizing Gorer's typology of styles of mourning. There were three major categories: little or no mourning, time-limited mourning, and unlimited mourning. Some of the large-scale factors that encourage one or the other pattern and give it its social meaning were discussed.

The distinction between public and private mourning is difficult to draw clearly. As members of a society, the public aspects of our lives have meaning for the private. We measure our careers in the role of the bereaved by standards provided by our community. We personalize them, but they remain socially rooted.

This chapter has been neither a condemnation nor a celebration of contemporary mourning practices. It has simply been an attempt to describe them and analyze the changes in their content and function. Although this is true of every chapter, it seems particularly important to make it explicit here. As the polemical quality of many "analyses" suggests, one is neutral in the face of mourning only with great difficulty.

Notes

1. At the other extreme, the absence or denial of mourning is sometimes accompanied by the immediate ridding from a house of all evidences of the deceased, as though they had never existed.

CHAPTER EIGHT
SUICIDE

The study of suicide, as Durkheim recognized, represents a fine opportunity to test the strength of sociology's analytical muscles. Suicide, on the surface the most personal of acts, takes place in a social context (Charmaz, 1980:233–380). It is subject to the influence of social, cultural, and economic forces as are all human behaviors. Culture, for example, provides the repertory of meanings from which suicidal individuals draw in choosing suicide over other alternatives.

Emile Durkheim (1951) adopted a macro perspective in his classic 1897 study, *Suicide*, attempting to confine his analysis to differences in overall rates of suicide from group to group. He very carefully excluded the intentions of the suicide victim from his definition because "Intent is too intimate a thing to be more than approximately interpreted by others. It even escapes self-observation" (Durkheim, 1951:43).

Most of the work in sociology on suicide done since Durkheim takes his work into account either by refining it or by criticizing it. Durkheim set the agenda for all subsequent study of suicide by separating two major questions: (1) *Why does a particular individual commit suicide?* and *(2) Why does the suicide rate vary from group to group?* The first is inseparable from the issue of intention. The second defines suicide as a *social fact,* that is, a property of a society or group rather than of any of the individuals who make up that society or group. Durkheim felt that you could not answer the second question by focusing on the first, and it was this second question that was the proper ground of sociology.

Psychologists have tended to address the first question, sometimes using their work to generalize about suicide rates. While sociologists have tended to address the second, some, such as Jack Douglas (1967), have insisted that the issue of intention (i.e., the meaning a suicidal act has for the individual) is crucial to understanding suicide as a social phenomenon.

SUICIDE RATES

Most attempts to explain variations in suicide rates have begun by criticizing official statistics on suicide. One type of criticism concerns the accuracy of those statistics (Atkinson, 1971:167). From this approach, the problem becomes assessing the effects of underreporting of suicide, refining the methods of collecting statistics, and so on. However, the meaning of suicide itself is taken for granted and so is the assumption on which the search for this "true" suicide rate is predicated: that the suicide rate can somehow be separated from the agencies who compile it and the methods they use.

The second and more radical criticism of official statistics takes the opposite position, that the first word (and, for some, the last word) on the suicide rate is the study of those responsible for producing it, for example, coroners and the police. This is an example of the approach to the social construction of reality discussed in Chapter Two.

Refining Durkheim's Work: Status Integration and the Suicide Rate

The extension of Durkheim's work that has received the most attention is Gibbs and Martin's (1964) theory of status integration. *Status integration* is the degree to which people in a group (or society) occupy the same set of statuses. If by knowing some of the statuses individuals occupy you can predict with a high degree of probability the other statuses those individuals occupy, the group has a high degree of status integration. In a simple village society, for example, if you know that someone is a 22-year-old male, you can predict with a high degree of probability that the person is also a husband, father, hunter, and member of a totem clan.

In a complex society such as the United States, knowing someone is a 22-year-old male would not allow you to make any predictions about other statuses with nearly as a high a degree of probability. In American society there are many, many status configurations. In other words, American society has a low degree of status integration.

The basic tenet of the theory of status integration is: "The suicide rate of a population varies inversely with the degree of status integration in that population" (Martin, 1968:80).

But, of course, the task of a theory is not simply to describe a relationship but to explain it. Why is a high degree of status integration associated with a low rate of suicide? The answer in part has to do with role conflict and the stress that it produces. In the village society just mentioned, role conflict is minimal. No one, for example, is likely to schedule a hunt on the same day as a totem clan meeting. People march in unison through their lives. In a complex society, role conflict is the normal order of things. A student only has to think of the stress that results from trying to juggle the demands of school, work, family, and friends to understand the appeal of the theory of status integration.

Another problem associated with a low degree of status integration is uncertainty. Relatively few status configurations means relatively few choices. Few choices means few decisions. In such a society, you avoid the stress of making bad decisions or painfully reaching no decisions. In sum, a society with high status integration may seem boring to Americans, but it is at least comfortably predictable.

The theory seems neatly to explain the approach, in the 1960s, of the suicide rate of women in the United States to the suicide rate of men. The ratio changed from 3.98 to 1 per 100,000 in 1954 to 2.46 to 1 in 1971 (McIntosh and Jewell, 1986:20 and passim). This period was characterized by the movement of women into the labor market and the turmoil of a redefinition of gender roles. In 1954, 26-year-old middle-class female would be combined with wife, mother, housewife, PTA member, and so on, with a higher degree of probability than any status configuration for 26-year-old middle-class female in 1971. In other words, the path for women in 1954 may have been confining by current standards, but it was more certain and secure; it may have meant fewer options, but it also meant fewer conflicts and fewer decisions and chances for mistakes.

The theory of status integration was an attempt to put Durkheim's notion of integration on a more solid empirical footing. However, evidence marshaled to support it has been short of overwhelming. Take the case of gender and suicide rates already mentioned. Since 1971, the discrepancy between the suicide rates for men and women has steadily grown (McIntosh and Jewell, 1986). While you could argue that only in the period of transition was a low degree of status integration present, these recent figures hardly constitute the support for Durkheim's theory that the earlier shift in rate did. In fact, a major analysis of data from the 1970 census, which Stafford and Gibbs (1985:63) described as the "most complete test of status integration ever undertaken," generally failed to support the theory. In sum, while the theory is far from dead, it is tottering badly.

Bypassing Durkheim's Work: The Social Construction of Suicide and the Suicide Rate

The more radical approach to studying the suicide rate focuses on how the suicide rate is "produced." It is based on the assumption that the meaning of suicide is problematic because it varies from historical period to historical period, among cultures, and even within one culture (Douglas, 1967:157). It is consequently important to study the process by which some deaths come to be defined as suicides. The focus shifts in some work from the person who commits suicide to the people who have the legitimate right to judge some deaths suicides and some deaths not, that is, coroners, the police, and so on. They in effect "produce" the suicide rate.

A major study in this tradition was done by J. Maxwell Atkinson (1971; 1978). He studied the rules that English coroners use to decide that some deaths are suicides and some deaths are not. Those often idiosyncratic guidelines fall into four categories. *Suicide notes* are taken as the surest sign, but are only left in a small percentage of cases. The *mode of death* is also taken as a fairly certain indication. For example, hanging is usually seen as good grounds for a suicide verdict. Automobile crash fatalities, on the other hand, are usually seen as accidents. Other modes of death are seen as more ambiguous and require the invocation of special rules. One coroner, for example, whose territory is a resort area, said, "A thing I look for in a drowning is whether or not the clothes are left folded. If they are found neatly folded on the beach, it usually points to a suicide" (Atkinson, 1971:179). A third guideline is the *location and circumstances of death.* Compare, for example, a barbiturate overdose taken in a bedroom as opposed to the woods. Or imagine someone, dead of gas fumes, in a kitchen with windows shut and towels stuffed under the doors (Atkinson, 1971:180).

The final tool in a coroner's determinations is *life history and mental condition.* As discussed in Chapters Two and Four, case histories are attempts to arrange "facts" to make sense out of some outcome. In coroner's inquests, the "facts" of the deceased's life are collected and arranged to see if they make more sense leading up to a suicidal outcome as opposed to a nonsuicidal outcome. "Happiness," as Atkinson (1971:181) notes, "is inconsistent with suicidal intent."

Even a cursory examination of these rules reveals how arbitrary they are and how arbitrarily they might be applied. A suicide note, as readers of Agatha Christie know all too well, is sometimes a cover-up for murder. Some people try to make their suicides in car crashes seem like accidents to allow their heirs to collect insurance. Neatly folded clothing can indicate an anal-compulsive swimmer. Some people certainly choose their bedrooms to commit suicide using drugs while others take drugs in isolated locations for the "high" (or "low"). In England, towels stuffed under the doors and windows tightly shut are sensible adaptations to modest central heating. Finally, the reconstruction of the deceased's life leading up to death is always fraught with difficulties (as readers of Edwin Arlington Robinson's "Richard Cory" are well aware).

In sum, it is clear that the study of how suicide rates are produced is both interesting in its own right and a necessary first step to using those statistics in analysis. With a better understanding of the precise limitations of those statistics, you can get on with the study of those who commit suicide (not simply those who monitor and tabulate those suicides).

Suicide and Intention

The focus on life history and mental condition reintroduced the notion of intention into the study of suicide. What sociology can contribute to the study of intention is the delineation of the cultural meanings a suicidal act might have and the values that are tied to those meanings. Trying to explain a suicide in the contemporary United States, where suicide is stigmatized and often seen as *prima facie* evidence of mental illness, is a very different matter from explaining a suicide in sixteenth-century Japan, where ritual suicide was seen as a rational attempt to restore honor to a dishonored life.

A major advocate of the focus on the social meanings of suicide is Jack Douglas (1967). Douglas (1967:154) claims that sociologists' taking Durkheim's work as their point of departure is instrumental "in preventing sociological investigations of the real-world cases of suicide and in continuing the uncritical use of official statistics." He sees suicide as an act of communication whose meaning varies. Suicide might be a way of moving the soul into the next world or transforming the self in the suicide's eyes and in the eyes of others. It might also be a method of revenge. To understand the meaning in a specific case, you would have to study the specific meanings that emerge in the suicide's interaction with others.

These "local" (319) meanings must of necessity be embedded in larger cultural meanings. (For example, in China suicide was a characteristic method of revenge.) It is these larger cultural meanings, some would maintain, that are the proper province of sociologists. Charmaz (1980:254–261), for one, suggests that the Protestant Ethos that emphasizes individual responsibility and control of yourself and your world results in fragmented social relationships. (This value scheme was discussed in Chapter Three in relation to attitudes toward death.) Failure to control other aspects of a person's life may lead to an attempt to control that one aspect. Suicide, in effect, becomes an attempt to bring death under control.[1] This of course is made more likely in a society whose structure gives its members less of a feeling of control over their lives. A mass society, a society in which impersonal bureaucratic structures are everywhere, and in which ideologies exist to clear the way for disowning your actions, is precisely that kind of society.

THE USE AND DISUSE OF SUICIDE STATISTICS

It would be bravado to attempt a glib solution to the complex problems, already discussed, in the study of suicide. However, to say that suicide statistics are suspect is not to say that they are incorrect. It is merely to recommend treating them with caution. By examining the method of their collection, it is possible to begin to control biases that affect them.

Another source of difficulty in the study of suicide is the practice of lumping all suicides together and trying to explain them as though they were the same. Atkinson (1978:24) mentions Alasdair Mac-Intyre's analogy of hole-diggers: "clearly it would be ludicrous to try to explain the digging of a hole to plant a rose bush and the digging of a hole to bury a murder victim by reference to the same theory of hole-digging." But sociologists studying suicide, says Atkinson, make precisely that error. If, however, you can begin separating suicides into categories that make analytic sense, you have at least begun to solve the problem. It is further helped by studying the repertory of meanings suicide has in a particular group, although the way specific individuals work up these culturally provided meanings will of course be idiosyncratic. You can, for example, study the meanings of suicide by determining how many suicide myths people subscribe to (McIntosh, Hubbard, and Santos, 1983) and how those myths affect interaction with suicidal individuals, or by studying the interaction between coroners' theories of suicide and sociological and popular theories of suicide (Atkinson, 1978).

In sum, awareness of the problems involved in studying suicide should lead to analytic humility, not analytic paralysis.

ADOLESCENT SUICIDE: A CASE STUDY OF STATISTICAL RATES AND SOCIAL MEANINGS

The suicide rate for adolescents in the United States has risen enough in the past twenty or so years and has received enough public attention to become, in Ronald Maris's (1985:91) words, "*the* issue in suicidology right now, as far as the general public is concerned." The suicide rate for ages 15 to 24 more than doubled from 1960 to 1980—a 237 percent increase (Maris, 1985:93)—and tripled from the mid-1950s to the mid-1980s (Mercy et al., 1984).

However, this increase alone is not sufficient to explain the public outcry. Between 1970 and 1980, the suicide rate for ages 25 to 34 rose almost 30 percent, compared to the 50 percent rise in the rate for ages 15 to 24 (Centers for Disease Control, 1985:28). In addition, the rate in 1982 for ages 75 to 84 was 20.3 per 100,000 while for ages 15 to 24, it was 12.1 per 100,000, down from 12.4 in 1979 (National Center for Health Statistics, 1984:19). Even the use of statistics for ages 15 to 24, when most of the publicity has focused on "teenagers" or "adolescents," reveals a value bias. If in fact the categories 15 to 19 and 20 to 24 are used, the increase from 1970 to 1980 for 15 to 19 is 43.5 percent versus 53.8 percent for 20 to 24 [under 15 remained the same (Centers for Disease Control, 1985:13)].[2]

The additional factor is the cultural view that there is something wrong with suicide in general and something terribly wrong with young people killing themselves. As Maris (1985:97) observed, "the loss of even one person so young seems unnecessary and tragic." In other words, one way culture impinges on adolescent suicide is by defining it as a critical problem.

Attempts to explain the overall rise in adolescent suicide must take into account the necessity of refining the general rate into workable analytical categories. One unified theory can't explain the rise in adolescent suicide any better than a single theory can explain the overall rate of suicide (Maris, 1985:104). The forces that are often cited to explain the increase, for example, violence in the media, drug abuse, the identity uncertainties of adolescence, affect all adolescents, but only a handful commit suicide. Obviously, factors mediate the effects of these forces, making some individuals more susceptible, some less susceptible, to their influence.

An adequate analysis of adolescent suicide would have to describe the cultural setting and other large-scale forces that affect adolescents. It would differentiate adolescents from other age categories, and adolescent suicide from other kinds of suicide. It would study the factors that mediate the influence of these large-scale forces, sorting out types of adolescent suicide in the process. Finally, it would delineate the changes that have taken place over the period under study; you obviously can't explain an increased rate by pointing to constants like the trauma of the adolescent years.

It would be nice to deliver an analysis like that after announcing its parameters. That is beyond the scope of this writer, this book, and, currently, this field. Instead, some suggestive work will be presented as a step in the right direction.

One example of large-scale factors that provide the setting for this increase is cultural values. The values that affect suicide in general, for example, the Protestant Ethos, also affect adolescents. However, in the case of adolescents, this notion of individual responsibility is set against a lack of real control over their destinies (almost all live at home, where the rules of their lives are set by adults). In addition, the notion of individual responsibility conflicts with deterministic ideologies that blame what happens to you on upbringing [what Strauss (1969:91) calls "variations on basic themes" models of development], on culture, on socioeconomic class, and the like. There is also a tendency to define what were formerly seen as moral crises as personal ones (Schur, 1976) and an age-graded self-centeredness, sometimes described as the "me generation." This conflict between I'm-not-to-blame and everything's-my-fault versions of responsibility and I'm-the-center-of-the-universe but I can't-make-anything-happen versions of control leads to guilt among the blameless and expectations of control among the helpless. Some research (e.g., Topol and Reznikoff, 1982) suggests that an external locus of control, the sense that forces outside yourself influence the events of your life, has a significant correlation with feelings of hopelessness and suicide attempts. The influence of this cultural strain on suicide is apparent.

Adolescence, never quite the same after the 1960s and early 1970s shifted the center of gravity of American culture to youth, is a particularly ambiguous age, not quite childhood, not quite adulthood. In addition, the boundaries of childhood are shifting to make the onset of adolescence earlier and earlier (Postman, 1982) and the definition of adolescence even more problematic. Adolescence also has no clear end. Bennett Berger (1969) captured this in the title of his article, "The New Stage of American Man—Almost Endless Adolescence." One consequence of this, Maris (1985:100) points out, is that adolescents are "shut out of meaningful participation in society . . . [while being subjected] to the pressures and stresses of living contingently for prolonged periods of time in an achievement-oriented society. . . . Little wonder then that young people in our society may have their own special set of social problems, including suicide."

As you might expect, while adolescent and adult suicide share some characteristics, there are noticeable differences. For example, adolescent suicides (in Maris's study, 1985:106) tend to be motivated more by interpersonal conflicts; involve more motives of revenge and feelings of anger; be more romantic and idealistic; result more from feelings of "prolonged uselessness, social postponement, and social disenfranchisement from meaningful participation in valued life activities, like marriage and a job"; and so on.

But, since all of the just-mentioned strains presumably affect all adolescents, why do only a few commit suicide? Conditions obviously mediate the influence of these forces. These conditions are personal and social. Personal characteristics and biographical details are crucial in moving a particular individual to suicide. Social factors are more appropriately studied sociologically. They constitute what Everett Hughes (1958) has called *career contingencies,* factors on which a person's movement along one path in a role as opposed to another depend. As discussed in Chapter Four, when people exposed to similar forces move along different paths, contingencies are operating. Contingencies may be seen as switches that move a life along one track instead of another.

Miller et al. (1984) and McIntosh and Jewell (1986) suggest that, in relation to the decline in the suicide rate of young white females, the availablility of suicide prevention centers and their greater use by this group may be important contingencies in a suicidal career.

Another contingency is the presence of role models for suicidal behavior. David Phillips (1974) studied the effect of the suicides of famous people that were reported on the front page of *The New York Times* on the overall rate of suicide in the month that followed. Of the 34 suicides reported on the front page of *The New York Times* from 1948 to 1967, 28 were followed by a rise in the suicide rate. Phillips called this the Werther effect after Goethe's *The Sorrows of Young Werther,* whose publication set off waves of youthful suicides in European cities. He later suggested that mention of suicides on television news programs had the same effect (Bollen and Phillips, 1982).

More recently, Wasserman (1984) reexamined Phillips's original data and concluded that other factors, for example, the business cycle, the occurrence of more prominent suicides in downswings of the economy, explained the rise in suicide rates Phillips attributed to imitation. There was, however, a significant exception, the suicides of celebrities. Wasserman suggests that this results from the greater publicity their deaths generate. It may also be true that the rate may rise in specific groups that identify with particular celebrities.

It seems safe to say that imitative suicides are more likely in groups, like adolescents, in which identity is more problematic and in which following someone in death seems a grim companion to following in the footsteps of a celebrity in life. In other words, adolescents, for whom fads have always been a means of attachment to something secure, are subject to imitation in suicide just as in dress. Certainly, imitation seemed to operate in the waves of regional suicides among high school students that sparked the most recent concern.

These contingencies, of course, don't make suicide inevitable, nor does their absence guarantee an absence of suicides. But they do place people in situations that open up suicide as an alternative. In addition, no one contingency may be sufficient to explain a suicide. A number may operate together.

Finally, to explain why the adolescent suicide rate has risen, you have to point to conditions that have changed. Most studies have focused on the forces that propel adolescents toward suicide. In a novel approach, Menno Boldt (1982–83) suggests that it may not be so much a matter of a strengthening of those forces as a weakening of resistance to them; that is, suicide has become a more acceptable alternative. In study of the attitudes toward suicide of high school students and members of their parents' generation in a Canadian city, Boldt found that his young sample saw suicide as a societal rather than as an individual failing, an act to which little stigma should be attached, and an act that eventuates in passage to heaven rather than hell. The older sample more often than the young sample saw suicide as an individual failing, to which somewhat more stigma should be attached, and as an act that would damn the suicide to hell.

For all the methodological difficulties in his study, Boldt's basic idea of the importance of shifts in the social meanings of suicide and death remains fascinating:

> Given that an individual always has several plausible courses of action open to him, along with some freedom of choice, the operative normative evaluations of suicide and death within a culture or subculture must be viewed as two of the most important and stable influences in a person's frame of reference regarding the suicidal option. (146)

The suicides of prominent figures, of course, may be interpreted as another way in which suicide can become more acceptable as an option.

SOCIOLOGY AND SUICIDE

Edwin Shneidman (1985:237–238) points to a possible pattern in the patchwork of suicides:

> If there are common psychodynamic themes in suicide, they probably relate to omnipotence and loss. In the unconscious, every suicide is psychodynamically related, directly or indirectly, to feelings of omnipotence-impotence; to feelings of being all-powerful and powerless-helpless. Suicide is an effort to do *something* effective, impactful, dramatic, memorable, noteworthy, special. . . . At the the moment of committing suicide, the individual may feel he controls the world—and by his death can bring it down. At least he controls his own destiny, and realistically typically touches and influences the destinies of at least several others.[3]

Opportunities for control in people's public and private lives are variably constricted in a society. Pressures build up and weigh differentially on people. Portraying these constrictions and pressures can sensitize us to look for their effects in the lives of individuals.

In the main, sociology has attempted to understand the broad contours of suicide in a society. Translating these trends and large-scale factors into terms that make an individual's everyday world and personal life comprehensible and into terms that are useful to people working to prevent suicides represents a promise largely unfulfilled. It is only when efforts are made to realize what C. Wright Mills (1959:3–24) called the promise of the sociological imagination—to understand "the intersections of biography and history (7)"—that sociology will make its greatest contribution to understanding and preventing suicide. When overall trends and social meanings are rooted in referents that are part of people's everyday lives, sociology will have utility in addressing individual suicides and suicidal individuals.

SUMMARY

It is obvious from this chapter that suicide is a complex social phenomenon. The confidence with which Durkheim cleanly split the sociological approach to suicide from the approaches of other disciplines seems hardly warranted.

That said, sociologists have tended to study suicide in its social context. On a macro level, this tendency has meant focusing on suicide rates. In one view, attempts are made to explain variations in those rates in terms of large-scale factors such as sex, age, and socioeconomic class. In an alternate view, suicide rates become data in the study of social construction. It is not so much their reliability as their validity that is at stake. However, if the study of suicide is not to become, first and last, the study of the compilation of official statistics, and never get around to the study of the behavior and people those statistics purport to describe, suicide statistics will have to be used, however cautiously. The goal is to study their compilation and question their validity *as a means of enhancing* their accuracy.

The intention of the individuals who kill themselves, which had been banished by Durkheim to the territory of psychology, has been reintroduced into sociology through the study of social meanings. These social meanings, worked up in idiosyncratic ways by specific individuals, are appropriate data for sociologists to study.

The sociological study of suicide involves the study of both changing rates and changing social meanings. It represents a fine tribute to Durkheim's work.

Notes

1. Compare this with David Bakan's (1969) notion that suicide is an attempt to achieve immortality, a course that might be less necessary if our society gave us a feeling of greater control over our lives and a greater prospect of theologically underwritten immortality.

2. For a more detailed analysis of the relationship between the statistics of adolescent suicide and their public interpretation, see Maris (1985).

3. Compare this with Mills's (1959:3) characterization of an individual's sense of control in modern mass society: "Nowadays men often feel that their private lives are a series of traps. They sense that within their everyday worlds, they cannot overcome their troubles, and in this feeling they are often quite correct: What ordinary men are directly aware of and what they try to do are bounded by the private orbits in which they live; their visions and their powers are limited to the close-up scenes of job, family, neighborhood; in other milieux, they move vicariously and remain spectators. And the more aware they become, however vaguely, of ambitions and threats which transcend their immediate locales, the more trapped they seem to feel."

CHAPTER NINE
NEAR-DEATH EXPERIENCES

People have an inexhaustible attraction to immortality. Notions of the survival of the spirit after death have usually been couched in religious terms. In the past fifteen or so years, the survival of the spirit after death has been addressed in the form of the study of near-death experiences. *Near-death experiences,* or NDEs, are the experiences some people report they have when they come close to clinical death. From this definition it is clear that not all people close to clinical death report these experiences, that people who have them are near death, but not dead, and that their significance is tied to particular definitions of clinical death (e.g., when NDEs are experienced, they are almost always associated with people whose hearts have stopped beating rather than with people whose EEGs are flat). In sum, NDEs are social constructions and must be seen in relation to the social and historical context in which they occur.

NDEs may be studied in at least two ways. First, they may be approached as phenomena to be described and explained. Second, the popularity of the idea and study of NDEs may also be examined. Although NDEs have been reported since ancient times (Moody, 1978:63–77) and studied for almost a hundred years (Audette, 1982:31), it is only in about the last fifteen years that popular interest in the United States has burgeoned and attempts have been made to establish a separate field to study NDEs, circumthanatology (Lundahl, 1982:xii). The questions of what is known about NDEs, how those findings can be explained, and why the topic has become so popular will make up a large portion of this chapter. First, it is important to clarify the issue of what research on NDEs can and cannot demonstrate.

The people who report these experiences are *near* to death, not dead. Consequently, what is being studied is what happens to some people who have come close to death, not people who have died and returned from the dead. The clinical definition used to decide that a person is dead is a social construction that varies over time. Although almost every case was "dead" according to the stopped-heartbeat definition of death, no one was dead using the more recent flat-EEG definition of death.

Although some researchers make claims to the contrary (Osis and Haraldsson, 1977), it seems obvious that the work of circumthanatologists, no matter how scientifically solid, will never answer definitively the question that moves most nonscientists interested in this area: Does the spirit survive after death? As Ring and Franklin (1981–82:204) commenting on the rare unpleasant aspects of some NDEs succinctly observe, "Needless to say, near-death research can never settle the question of whether there is a hell any more than its findings can prove the existence of any sort of afterlife." Researchers study people who have *almost* left this world, not people who have returned from some afterworld.

STUDIES OF NEAR-DEATH EXPERIENCES

Description of NDEs

Most recent work on NDEs traces it roots back to Raymond Moody's (1976) *Life after Life,* first published in 1975. Moody studied about 150 people who had what he termed "near-death experiences." He noticed common elements in their accounts and constructed a model of the prototypical near-death experience consisting of eleven components.[1] These elements were ineffability, hearing the news, feelings of peace and quiet, the noise, the dark tunnel, out of the body, meeting others, the being of light, the review, the border or limit, and coming back. Moody claimed that the experiences usually occurred in the sequence listed and that the closer to death a person came, the greater number of these stages were passed. The overall experience was somewhere between pleasant and ecstatic.

While Moody's work was suggestive, it wasn't systematic. As Kenneth Ring (1980:19) put it, Moody's data were not "presented in a form that renders them susceptible to scientific analysis and evaluation." In fact, most of the work that followed the publication of *Life After Life,* including Ring's, is an attempt to make Moody's work credible to medical, behavioral, and social scientists. Ring, for example, carefully studied 102 people who had come close to death to determine how many had what Moody called a "near-death experience" or in Ring's more precise term a "core experience" (more precise because, although all 102 had come near death, only 49 had experiences close enough to what Moody described to warrant calling them "core experiencers").

Ring developed an index to measure how intense a core experience each subject had. Using this index, he broke his sample into three groups: nonexperiencers (53 or 52 percent), moderate experiencers (22 or 22 percent), and deep experiencers (27 or 26 percent).[2] Supporting Moody's overall findings, Ring concluded that experiences arranged themselves into five stages, although not all subjects passed through all five. These stages are: (1) the affective component: peace and the sense of well-being; (2) body separation: leaving the body behind; (3) entering the darkness; (4) seeing the light; and (5) entering the light (Ring, 1980:39–66). Running parallel to the three intermediate stages, a decision-making process on whether or not to return to life is begun that eventuates in the "return to life." This usually takes place between the third and fourth stages. The elements of this decision-making process include the life review, the encounter with a "presence," the encounter with deceased loved ones, and making the decision (67–68).

Ring found that the proportion passing through each of the five stages decreased steadily, from 60 percent for the initial state (peace), to 37 percent (body separation), to 23 percent (entering the darkness), to 16 percent (seeing the light), to only 10 percent for the final stage (entering the light) (40). Although offered as a tentative conclusion, he also claimed that the probability of having a core experience to any stage was not significantly correlated with socioeconomic class, religiosity, familiarity with work on the near-death experience, or the manner of nearly dying.

On the whole, the emotional quality of the core experience was decidedly positive, a finding of almost all near-death studies. As Ring (1982:121) wrote, "there is a consistent and dramatically positive emotional response to apparent near-death by core experiencers . . . the core experiencers often report feelings of peace as well as a transcendent sense of well-being."

However, there are exceptions reported in a few studies. Garfield (1979) interviewed thirty-six patients who had come close to death. Half reported NDEs of various sorts. Of those, only seven reported the pleasant "core experience" Ring described. Four, on the other hand, had frightening visions. In addition, two had hazier experiences with at least some unpleasant aspects.

In addition to variations in the emotional quality of the NDEs, some studies have reported variations in the content of the experience. A study by Osis and Haraldsson (1977) compared Indian and American physicians' and nurses' reports of death-bed visions of terminally ill patients. They studied reports of "hallucinations" (as they called them) of nearly five hundred patients. The most common vision was of human figures usually appearing to help the patient into the next world. However, Americans typically saw deceased people, while Indians typically saw figures with religious significance. In a characteristically American way, few apparitions came to take American patients into the next world against their will. On the other hand, about one quarter of the apparitions appearing to Indian patients came to take them away against their will. These also accounted for most of the cases with unpleasant emotions attached to them. Otherwise, as with most studies, the emotional tenor of the experience was generally positive.

In sum, studies to date seem to indicate that many, but not most, people who have come near to death have "near-death experiences," most NDEs have a common pattern, but with significant variations, and most NDEs generate pleasant feelings but some are emotionally terrible.

Explanations of NDEs

As is usual with science, describing something is much easier than explaining it. The problems in explaining NDEs center on how universal the experience is. First, if not all people have them, is there anything special about people who do? If, for example, you could show that only people who were deeply religious and believed strongly in an afterlife and the ability to glimpse it in this life had NDEs, you would be reasonably sure that the experience had more to do with the people and their beliefs than with the world. Second, if not all people have them but there is nothing special about the people who do, what explains NDEs when they do occur?

Of course, research into NDEs is difficult at best (Kamerman, 1984). A researcher must currently rely entirely on the self-report of subjects (whether firsthand as in the case of Ring, or secondhand as in the case of Osis and Haraldsson).[3] Those self-reports are after the fact, sometimes much later than the experience. This makes them subject to all the possible distortions of experiences recalled (Thomas, Cooper, and Suscovich, 1982–83). The very popularity of accounts of near-death experiences may have an unfortunate consequence for researchers. It will be increasingly difficult to know for certain whether subjects are using Raymond Moody's prototypical near-death experience as a corset, that is, to squeeze their experiences into the proper form. In addition, the systematic study of NDEs is a relatively recent development preceded and surrounded by popular, impressionistic, or pseudoscientific rambles.

It is clear from the research that does exist that not all people who come close to death have NDEs. Robert Kastenbaum (1981:293) takes this as one sign that NDEs have nothing necessarily to do with death. If they did you would expect all people coming close to death to have them, which they don't. In addition, Kastenbaum (1981:294) claims, out-of-body experiences resembling the typical NDE are had by people in other than near-death situations, for example, during psychedelic drug use. He concludes that "there appears little reason to accept the current spate of NDEs as demonstrating anything about the death state per se, or about the possibility of survival" (294). And, he adds, even if the evidence did add up to the survival after death (which he claims it doesn't), it wouldn't necessarily mean that survival would be permanent.

The fact that the content of NDEs is tied to culture not only undermines the claim to universality, but also ties the experience to this world rather than the "next." While a pluralistic afterlife is possible, these variations in content so closely tied to distinctions in this world do cast suspicion on NDEs' being out of this world. This is the counterpart of the claim of many NDE researchers that the common features of NDEs demonstrate that they couldn't have anything to do with this world alone.

Kastenbaum acknowledges that even if NDEs have nothing to do with survival of the spirit after death, they still have to be explained. In attempting to provide an alternative to otherworldly and paranormal explanations, Kastenbaum mentions the work of Noyes and Kletti (1976) on *depersonalization*. They point out that in the face of threats to life, people sometimes detach themselves psychologically in rather extreme ways from their situations. This gives their perception of the world an aura of strangeness, gives them a sense of detachment from their bodies, and in some other ways produces phenomena characteristic of core experiences. Sabom and Kreutziger (1982:156) and Ring (1980:207–208), however, point out that core experiences differ in some respects from depersonalization. For example, depersonalization in patients described in earlier work in psychiatry was accompanied by a perceptual flatness whereas NDEs are accompanied by perceptual intensity.

Ring (1980), after rejecting alternative physiological and psychological explanations, concludes that NDEs represent true out-of-body experiences that transport a person into "the fourth-dimensional world" (234). With a caution that this idea is only tentative, Ring concludes that NDEs rest on the fact that "consciousness . . . may function independently of the physical body" (233).

From this sampling of conflicting views, it is clear that to date, although the occasionally mystical explanations offered by many NDE researchers are certainly not definitive, explanations offered by their critics are also problematic. As Sabom and Kreutziger (1982:158) succinctly put it, "The NDE cannot be adequately explained at the present time."

The Effects of NDEs

Another course that research has taken is the study of what happens to people after they report a core experience. One study of hospital patients (Sabom and Kreutziger, 1982) found that NDEs tended to reduce fears of death and intensify belief in an afterlife. Some terminally ill patients were able to handle their condition better because of the reduction of fear of death.

One of the most interesting aspects studied so far concerns the effects of NDEs on people who have attempted suicide. Ring and Franklin (1981–82) studied thirty-six people who had attempted suicide and felt they had come close to death. Most of the sample volunteered, in response to newspaper advertisements asking for suicide attempters to participate in a study. About half (seventeen) had had NDEs. While not all experienced every feature of the core experience, for example, only four encountered a "presence," pleasant emotional experiences were reported by all subjects.

This raises an interesting ethical issue concerning the relationship between NDEs and suicide. Edwin Shneidman (1973:61–70) suggests that the deromanticization of death may be one factor in encouraging some people to choose suicide. In the same way, Boldt (1982–83) claims that the rise in the rate of adolescent suicide may be more a function of removing barriers to suicide than of an increase of forces propelling young people toward the barriers. If Shneidman and Boldt are correct, publicizing a pleasant view of death, certainly one of the latent functions of near-death research (or at least popular literature on near-death research) is almost to encourage suicide. As Ring and Franklin (1981–82:205) admit, "Although, as we have said, near-death research can obviously never *prove* there is a life after death, much less that the life is always an improvement over earthly life, it is obvious that near-death research *does* tend to convey a very positive idea of a possible afterlife."

However, Ring and Franklin found that one effect of an NDE associated with a suicide attempt was a diminution of suicidal intent and a willingness to "counsel others *against* suicide despite (or, perhaps one should say, because of) having had a beautiful suicide-related NDE themselves" (206). In a partial justification of continued NDE research based on its utility in suicide prevention, they conclude, "Thus, if suicidal individuals pay heed to the real authorities—those who have been there—the result of publicizing these suicide-related NDEs should actually serve to deter rather than to promote suicide attempts" (206).

There are, of course, limitations to this point of view. The overwhelming majority of people who read about NDEs don't read about them in journals like *Omega,* where Ring and Franklin's work was published. Rather, they read popular magazines or bestsellers like Moody's *Life After Life,* which has sold over three million copies. Consequently, it is likely that the overwhelming majority of suicide-prone people who learn about NDEs hear the "good news" in the same manner. It is conceivable that when you are pointed in the direction of suicide anyway, the promise of peace, light, and happy reunions may be the tailwind in your flight. In addition, the decision-making process in the core experience may give suicidal people, many of whom only "gamble with death" (Shneidman, 1973), the illusion that they can change their minds even after they "die."

This is an ethical issue raised, but of course not settled, by NDE research. It reflects no more on the validity of that research than does the extensive coverage of the subject in popular magazines and tabloid newspapers. The widespread media coverage of NDEs is itself an interesting topic for analysis.

THE POPULARITY OF THE STUDY OF NEAR-DEATH EXPERIENCES

Explaining the popularity of an idea has no necessary consequences for judging the idea's validity. However, since the attractiveness of an idea varies between cultures and across time, it does have to be explained. As mentioned earlier, NDEs have been reported and recorded throughout history. It is only since the mid-1970s, however, that they have become a popular topic both in and out of the sciences. The publication of Raymond Moody's *Life After Life* in 1975 certainly sparked general interest in the subject. But its reception was itself a product of prior conditions. The reputation of an idea changes. Albert Heim's study of NDEs, for example, first published in 1892, "lay forgotten until interest in it was revived in the early 1970s" (Ring, 1980:21).

Moody (1976:145) suggests that NDEs are probably more common now than in the past because of medical advances. People who would certainly have died before can now sometimes be revived. Even if this were the case, that doesn't explain why the subject became popular. Death itself, a constant throughout history, has had its ups and downs as a topic of discussion and study.

The surge in NDE studies may be in part a by-product of the shift from a sacred to a secular view of death. With the questioning, and, for many, the disappearance of some traditional notions of an afterlife, the "scientifically" demonstrable existence of a secular afterworld has an obvious attraction. It is a thoroughly modern denial of the finality of death. In addition, it suggests that death is generally a pleasant experience. There are bright lights, people waiting for you, and so forth. A final attraction is the element of choice. It puts death under your control. In a larger sense, all the factors that operated to stimulate interest in the topic of death in general also operated to stimulate interest in the near-death experience.

SUMMARY

Near-death experiences are the experiences some people report they have when they come close to clinical death. This definition suggests that not all people near death have them, and that people who have them are only *near* to death; that is, they haven't died and come back. Consequently, near-death research has nothing necessarily to do with the survival of the spirit after death.

Although reports of near-death experiences have been made since ancient times, current research usually dates its beginnings from the 1975 publication of Raymond Moody's *Life After Life*. Research by physicians, psychologists, and social scientists since then has attempted to clarify and systematically ground Moody's work.

Moody described a prototypical NDE in which people left their bodies, traveled into a bright light, and entered "another" world populated with people who had already died. Ring suggested that specific stages characterize this core experience and that people who returned passed through each stage with decreasing frequency; that is, the fewest actually "entered" the light.

The major argument of most NDE researchers is that the experience has a common configuration that transcends cultural, historical, religious, and socioeconomic differences; that is, it is universal. Critics of these researchers point out that no one has explained why not everyone who comes close to death has an NDE, that some people have "NDEs" who haven't come close to death, and that there *is* some variation in the accounts, cross-culturally, historically, and in relation to social characteristics. Most (but not all) researchers agree that whatever the validity of the NDE as a concept, it has nothing necessarily to do with the survival of the spirit after death.

Another area of research focuses on the aftereffects of NDEs. Some studies indicate that people who have the core experience lose their fear of death. One study suggested that people who make serious suicide attempts, nearly die, and have NDEs, lose their desire to kill themselves. This touches on ethical issues in such research: Will promoting a pleasant picture of death tip suicidal individuals into suicide and, if so, should that possibility have any effect on the continuation of such research? The issues are far from clear although those who argue in terms of the beneficial effects of NDEs on suicide candidates are on shaky ground.

Finally, the popularity of the topic of NDEs was briefly discussed. Moody's book had something to do with it, but the popularity of Moody's book in turn rested on prior conditions. After the abandonment by many of traditional views of an afterlife, this secular, "scientifically based" view of a pleasant afterworld that can, to some degree, be turned down was extremely attractive. All the factors that increased public attention to death also worked to increase interest in NDEs.

But however appealing studies of NDEs may be, they can never do what in our private moments we would have them do: settle the question of whether death, in Herman Feifel's words, is a wall or a doorway (1959:xii).

Notes

1. Descriptions by his subjects included four additional features in the aftermath of the NDE: telling others, effects on lives, new views of death, and corroboration (Moody, 1976:84–101).

2. "Nonexperiencers" included some who had a small part of the core experience, but not " 'enough' of an experience to qualify as a 'core experiencer' " (Ring, 1980:33).

3. There are rare cases where a subject having an NDE "meets" the apparition of a dead person whose death is unknown to the subject. This is taken by some (e.g., Grosso, 1982:209) as possible evidence of a paranormal component of NDEs, "a kind of transworld ESP." Of course, since Osis and Haraldsson (1977) found that both living and dead persons appeared in NDEs, the significance of these rare cases as proof of a world beyond is undercut.

CHAPTER TEN
THE DEATH OF PETS

Because animals are often invested with human traits, the death of pets represents an opportunity to study the attitudes and behaviors toward human death discussed earlier in this book. In some cases, these attitudes appear in an even more salient form. For example, if mourning for a close friend is given little social support compared to mourning for almost any family member (as discussed in Chapter Six), then mourning for a pet exposes the hierarchy of legitimate grief even more clearly. If spending money for lavish funerals, caskets, cemetery plots, and the like for dead relatives has come under attack, then spending money for similar goods and services for pets is usually considered somewhere between bizarre and pathological.

There are also sociological issues that are clarified by examining the death of pets. For example, the process by which human traits are attributed to animals is a fine example of the process of social construction. The traits we select and the ones we neglect are influenced by social values (Ball, 1971).

Studying the death of pets is important for another reason. The death of a pet often represents a child's first experience with death. The stance taken by parents colors a child's attitude toward the human death he or she encounters later. This analogy is often consciously promoted by parents as the clearest way of explaining human death to children.

For these reasons and because of the larger point they make, that American attitudes toward pets and toward the death of pets reflect larger currents in American culture, that is, are productions of American culture just as certainly as conceptions of the afterlife, the subject of this chapter is a significant area in the sociological analysis of death.

THE SOCIAL CONSTRUCTION OF ANIMAL CHARACTER: THE PET AS A FAMILY MEMBER

To understand the "interaction" between people and pets, you must first understand how people see those pets. It is a basic idea of the sociological approach to interaction that people need to identify, and identify with those with whom they communicate and interact before that communication and interaction can take place (Stone and Farberman, 1981:2–11). It is understandable that people living in close quarters with pets would want to attribute recognizable human traits to them, both to make them comprehensible and to make interaction with them seem reasonable. The tendency of people to want to do this is probably related to the range of their other social contacts. If a person is elderly and living alone except for a pet, the pet may be the only, or at least the major, source of companionship (Bikales, 1975; Quackenbush, 1984).

People seem always to have attributed human traits to animals. As Boyce Rensberger (1978:1) has written about wild animals:

> In total ignorance of their real traits, humans have attributed to many animals a variety of human traits in the ideal or extreme. Lions are noble. Wolves are ruthless and savage. Peacocks are vain. Hyenas are slinking cowards. Songbirds are cheerful. Eagles are proud and watchful.

The fact, according to Rensberger, that these myths have little basis in reality, for example, the lion is "lazy, murderous" (2), a scavenger rather than a hunter, tells much more about people and their needs than about animals and their natures.

The same, of course, is true of household pets. Donald Ball (1971) points out that the traits that are attributed to dogs and cats are rooted in differences in the social organization and social behavior of those animals. For example, cats (except for lions) hunt alone with short bursts of energy. They tend to hunt prey smaller than themselves; they are solitary eaters as well as solitary hunters. "Survival, then, does not encourage collective action" (Ball, 1971:45). For that reason, cats are seen as "independent." Dogs, who in nature hunt in packs, are seen as sociable. Cats, because "their persistence for food is short, albeit intense . . . are difficult to train" (45). While Ball predicts that domestic cats will eventually lose this "independence" because cats who purr and curl up in their owners' laps have an edge in the process of natural (i.e., pet owners') selection, the point remains that attributed traits are chosen and differentially valued on human grounds. Ball sums up the convoluted quality of human interpretations of animal character by saying,

> Cats are not more independent than dogs in a characterological sense— often spoken of as a virtue when applied to humans—they are simply less social in a relational sense—paradoxically, often spoken of as a blemish when attributed to humans. (47)

To the extent to which pets are seen as human, their deaths are mourned as human deaths. The real question in the social construction of animal character is *to what extent are pets seen as human?* One way of focusing this question is to examine the relationships of people and their pets. To what extent and in what ways are pets treated as members of the family? And which members are they treated like? The answers to these questions are deceptively simple. Pets are called "family members" by some, are treated like family members in some ways and not in others, and when they are, they are usually treated like perpetual children (Quackenbush, 1985:395).

These questions are obviously more complex. Lucy Jen Huang Hickrod and Raymond L. Schmitt (1982) examined in detail the social construction of the pet as a family member. Pets are *like* family members in many respects:

> Pets are named, fed, groomed, photographed, talked to, protected, and mourned. Owners sleep and play with pets. They give them birthday parties and attribute human characteristics to them. (59)

People talk to their pets as though their pets understood the language (61). This goes beyond simply giving them commands; it often resembles a conversation.

Pet owners commonly interpret the behavior of pets in human terms. Pets are defined as loyal, in fact more constant in their loyalty than people (63). This is expressed by saying that although husbands or wives leave us, animals get lost. Because we provide the meaning of pets' behavior, we have greater latitude in interpreting it. Pets won't argue with us about the meaning of their actions (in fact, they don't argue with us about anything). Because of this amiability, because pets are dependent on us for their lives, particularly after their domestication is complete, and because unlike children pets remain dependents throughout their lives, people often develop strong attachments to their pets. They are considered quasi-family members (Hickrod and Schmitt, 1982:67) and are treated accordingly. They "take on a particular social status (that of family member) and have fairly well-prescribed social roles in any given family (that of a child-like member)" (Quackenbush, 1985:395).

On the other hand, while their definition and treatment may be like those of a human family member, they are also different in important respects. As Hickrod and Schmitt (1982:71) put it, "The 'pet' is only 'almost human.'" People are reminded that their pets are considered animals by many in several ways. Hickrod and Schmitt point to several examples of the constraints on seeing pets as family members. "No Pets Allowed" signs tell pet owners that their pets are animals no matter how "civilized" pet owners think they are (65). However, "No Children Allowed" signs perform the same function although this doesn't imply that their status as family members is in doubt. Pets sometimes commit acts that are outrageous by human standards, for example, touching their own feces (66). Again, so do children to the constant embarrassment of their parents. In addition, "People have been rebuked for treating pets too much like family members" (59). This is certainly true and to that extent is an indication of how common such treatment is. Finally, some animals never become pets. They remain purely animals, for example, watchdogs kept outdoors (67). But, occasionally, family members, the very young or the very old, are treated in inhuman ways. These qualifications don't mean that animals are furry or feathered people. They mean instead that the differences between pets and people, at least as far as social definition and interaction, are matters of degree, that is, quantitative rather than qualitative. Pets are less welcome, more often outrageous, and more commonly treated like animals than children. On the other hand, you cannot understand the grief, bereavement, and mourning of some people on the death of their pets unless you understand the extent to which they are seen and treated as human.

To summarize, while in a strict sense pets aren't human, they are sometimes treated as though they were. And, while in a strict sense people aren't animals (at least not in the sense in which "animal" is meant here), they also are sometimes treated as though they were.

THE DEATH OF PETS: DEATH

As with human death, the course of pets' dying follows either quick-dying or lingering trajectories. Quick-dying trajectories are often the result of accidents or poisoning. In those cases, pet owners may flail themselves with guilt (Quackenbush, 1985:398). This is true in greater part because animals are defined as child-like. When they grow old, they are accorded treatment similar to that of some of the human elderly; that is, they are still (or as in the case of people, again) dealt with like children. Consequently, some of the same attitudes that are true for the death of children are true for the death of pets, although again, not as commonly or usually as intensely. When a child or childlike pet dies, parents or "parents" feel particularly responsible.

Lingering trajectories present special problems in pet deaths. In human deaths, although this is slowly changing, and in some countries such as Holland has for all intents and purposes changed, euthanasia is not a legal option. In animal deaths, however, euthanasia is a common and socially acceptable option. This acceptability doesn't necessarily make it an easy choice emotionally. In one sense it makes it more difficult. If the choice is between a slow painful death and euthanasia, a person has little discretion with human dying. With pets, the choice is entirely the owner's. The law performs no guilt-carrying function (Goffman, 1961:144). The pet's death is entirely the owner's responsibility, and the law can't be seen as the barrier that prevented a person from alleviating the suffering of a loved one as it can with human beings.

A pet's life span is relatively brief. For the most common pets, dogs, cats, and many birds, the span is roughly ten to twenty years. Because the opportunity for children and adolescents to witness death has diminished during this century due to increased life expectancy and the shift of the scene of death to institutions, the death of a pet frequently represents a child's or adolescent's first experience with death. The death of pets fulfills the function that a higher infant mortality rate, a shorter life expectancy, and a more even distribution of death across age groups used to perform. The way in which a pet's death is handled influences later interpretations of death. Just as parents are advised not to tell children that dead grandparents have "gone on a trip," the same caution is suggested in discussing a pet's death. One popular authority on pets, for example, advises parents to be honest and to avoid stories about trips, sleep, and willful flight (Caras, 1982).

Pet's lives sometimes coincide with specific periods and relationships in people's lives and consequently come to stand for those periods and relationships. The death of a childhood pet may symbolize the end of childhood. If a pet comes to stand for an individual who dies or a relationship that is terminated, the death of the pet who was the last living link to that past may promote acceptance of the loss of that individual or relationship. As Quackenbush and Glickman (1983:387) observe, "the death of the pet seems to signify and finalize the death of the person."

Just as a society's family structure affects reactions to human death, the same is probably true for reactions to the death of pets. People who live alone tend to be hit harder by the death of a companion pet than are people who live in large families (Quackenbush and Glickman, 1983:381). In general, the larger the family, the less the loss of one of its members disrupts the family's functioning and emotional life. In relation to family animals, Cusack and Smith (1984:41) point out that a pet functions as a "social lubricant":

> An animal not only promotes conversation and a common bond among a populace in a given environment, but it also facilitates social interaction with strangers, and thus can encourage new friendships and associations for the pet owner. (42)

Quackenbush (1984:297) speculates that pet deaths will become more difficult to handle as family size decreases, because "animal-owner relationships [will] become more dependent." Although he refers to elderly pet owners, the same would of course be true of anyone living alone, including younger single pet owners. The meaning of the death of pets is responsive to changes in the social structure of society just as the meaning of pets is influenced by cultural definitions and values and social context in general. Summarizing explanations of the positive value placed on pets in America, Hickrod and Schmitt (1982:71–72) mention factors that include "the history of animal domestication . . . [and] the emergence of an equalitarian view of pets and humans . . . [and this positive value] is sustained by the marketplace . . . , the media, advertisements . . . , 'pet heroes,' . . . [and] the interchangeability of animal and human words."

There are of course other factors influencing the social valuation of animals. While being positively valued and seen as humanlike (e.g, American racehorses being called "he" or "she" whereas British racehorses are called "it"), they are also symbols of status: purebreds versus "mutts," dogs for men versus dogs for women, upper-class breeds versus middle-class breeds. They are subject to shifting currents of fashion. They sometimes represent a considerable financial investment. A few are famous and worth a great deal of money; most are not. Functions and the bases of fame change, from war dogs and messenger pigeons to movie stars and drug-and-bomb–sniffing dogs. All these meanings affect the meaning of animals and, consequently, the power of their deaths to move us. Once again, to understand American death, you must understand American life.

THE DEATH OF PETS: GRIEF AND BEREAVEMENT

To the extent to which pet owners grieve, their grief resembles grief over human deaths. The symptoms in pet owners' grief are almost identical with the symptoms Lindemann (1944) described as being normal for grief in human deaths: among them are guilt, anger (Quackenbush, 1981:765), and alterations of normal patterns of conduct (Quackenbush, 1984:295; Quackenbush and Glickman, 1984:43). Grief work is also necessary in the death of a pet, although the duration and intensity of grief are probably not the same in most cases as for human death (Quackenbush, 1981:767). The availability of cheap and plentiful "substitutes" makes bringing grief work to closure more likely. In human death, while substitution is an ultimate alternative (people remarry, have or adopt new children), it is vastly more difficult. The complexity of our involvement with other people makes emotional replacement extremely problematic. To the extent to which we see humanlike personality in our pets, we have a similar problem replacing our pets. It is clear that differences in grieving are also qualitative more than quantitative, but they are differences nonetheless.

Delayed grief, anticipatory grief, displaced grief, and pathological grief are found in reactions to pet deaths as well as to human

deaths. When pets come to stand for people in the minds of their owners, for example, when the pet is the last vestige of a marriage broken
by death, the pet's death may become the object of displaced grief for
the dead husband or wife. This is the equivalent in death of the displaced affection people sometimes feel toward pets in life. Some people
who find it too threatening or complicated to love people love their pets
instead. Although this doesn't change the fact that most people love
pets for their own sakes, it does help to explain the comment made
about some pet owners that they love their pets more than they love
their children. Similarly, pets sometimes become the objects of the in-
dulgences we cannot allow ourselves or others around us. They are
sometimes, for example, overfed surrogates for diet-conscious Americans.

Therapists who work with bereaved pet owners report cases of
both delayed grief and what Lindemann (1944) called distorted reactions. Quackenbush and Glickman (1984:44–45) found what they term
"prolonged grieving" in 3 percent of the bereaved pet owners referred
to them for help. Two weeks after their pets' deaths,

> They had not returned to work, remained housebound, were preoccupied
> with thoughts of the dead animal, and showed increasing signs of depres-
> sion, such as insomnia, anorexia, withdrawal, and aural hallucinations.
> Their emotional responses—for example, anger, guilt, and denial—were
> both prolonged and maintained at high levels of intensity.

One reason suggested by Quackenbush (1985:397) for these reactions is the societal definition of bereavement for pets as nonlegitimate. If traditional mourning rituals for human deaths are being questioned, they are virtually nonexistent for pet deaths. When people do
engage in formal mourning for a pet, their behavior is considered
strange. This difficulty in finding an outlet for grief doesn't come so
much from the lack of rituals, as Quackenbush (1985:397) suggests, as
from the view of pets that underlies the dearth of mourning rituals.
The death of a pet would be a low-grief-expectation death (discussed in
Chapter Six). In the eyes of most people, we have no formal relationship with our pets, at least as "relationship" is defined in the human
sense, and are consequently not expected to grieve. These circumstances create a group of what Fudin and Devore (n.d.) call "the
unidentified bereaved," people who feel bereaved but, because they
have no legitimate claim to that status, are denied the grieving opportunities of the bereaved role. "Nonlegitimate" is a judgment expressed
in such remarks as, "What are you so upset about? It was only a bird."
This produces "an 'invisible' population with real psychological needs
[which] is currently being neglected and ignored" (Quackenbush and
Glickman, 1983:389).

An exception to this nonlegitimate bereavement status is made in the case of famous and valuable animals. When Smokey the Bear died in 1976, he was accorded the tributes, expressions of sadness, and ceremonies befitting a minor hero. Smokey had been found by rangers in a park in New Mexico in 1950, the injured survivor of a forest fire. He was installed in the National Zoo in Washington, D.C. and became the symbol and "voice" of the government campaign to prevent forest fires. He was also a major attraction at the zoo. His death was mentioned in all the media. He was buried in the park where he had been found (renamed the Smokey Bear Historical State Park).

A week later a memorial service was held at the park. About two hundred fifty attended, including schoolchildren who had been given the day off for the ceremony. Rites included group prayer, singing, and a eulogy by Elliot S. Barker who was game warden in the park when Smokey was found.

The important point here is that the bereavement of many Americans on the death of a bear whose likeness had adorned posters, who had made television commercials for a good cause, whose name, in addition to being a household word, had become the CB code word for policemen, and who was a star attraction at the National Zoo, was understandable in social terms, that is, was not considered strange or pathological.

THE DEATH OF PETS: MOURNING

As with grief and bereavement, mourning for pets is similar in form to mourning for people, but is usually different in scale and in the way it is interpreted by others.

Similar options are open for the disposal of human and animal remains. Quackenbush (1985:401) lists the options for pets as cremation, burial in a pet cemetery, private disposal of the body by owners, and leaving the body with a veterinarian for disposal and/or autopsy. The major difference between pet and human disposal is the fact that leaving the body for disposal is the most common choice for pets and burial in a cemetery is the most common pattern for humans. This again is a significant quantitative but not qualitative difference (human bodies are sometimes unclaimed or left with the funeral director for disposal).

Although they are vastly fewer in number than human cemeteries, there are about five hundred pet cemeteries in the United States (Hickrod and Schmitt, 1982:67); the oldest, the Hartsdale Canine Cemetery in Hartsdale, New York, was established in 1896. Many of the goods and services available in human cemeteries are available in pet

cemeteries, for example, caskets, monuments, flowers, plot maintenance, and perpetual care plans.

The trends that are true of human funerals have their counter-
parts in animal funerals. To the extent to which burial of a pet has
become ritualized, it has, as with human burials, become deritualized.
One authority on pets advises owners not to spend money on caskets,
plots, or headstones, but instead to donate the money to a humane society (Caras, 1982:78).

Memorialization is somewhat more acceptable for pet heroes.
They are valued according to standards similar to those used for human heroes, for example, loyalty, courage, success, and celebrity.
There are war memorials to war dogs such as the War Dog Memorial
at Hartsdale Canine Cemetery. The Peavey Fountain in Minneapolis,
which was originally a drinking fountain for horses, was rededicated
as a memorial to the horses who died in action in World War I. The
attribution of "superhuman" qualities to animals is obvious in the epitaph President John Tyler composed for his favorite horse:

> Here lies the body of my good horse, The General. For twenty years he
> bore me around the circuit of my practice, and in all that time he never
> made a blunder. Would that his master could say the same. (Wallis,
> 1973:245–46)

Private mourning for pets resembles that for humans. In both
cases, usual patterns of conduct are altered. Routines are disrupted.
People' lives are no longer punctuated and regularized by the necessity
of feeding a cat or taking a dog for a walk. Some bereaved pet owners
cut themselves off from others, take time off from work, and so forth
(Quackenbush and Glickman, 1984:43–44).

There are styles of mourning over pet loss that resemble those for
human loss, although once again, their frequency, intensity, and importance in a person's life are probably different. Quackenbush and
Glickman (1983:388) report cases of mummification. A few pet owners
they worked with continued to put out food and water for their animals
for some time after the pets died. At the other extreme, people sometimes rid their lives of every trace of the dead animal. In an advice col-
umn written for children by children, which appears in a Long Island
newspaper, a bereaved young girl whose kitten was "put to sleep" after
having been hit by a car was advised to throw out or put out of sight
every object associated with the kitten (*Newsday*, 1982:n.p.). (The
child was also advised to cry as much as she wanted, not to feel guilty,
and eventually to consider getting another kitten.)

As with bereavement, a major difference in the mourning for pets
is the interpretation made of it by others. Just as bereavement is usually defined as nonlegitimate, so is mourning. Not only is mourning for

pets subject to the same cultural constraints as mourning for humans, but it bears the additional burden of nonlegitimacy. This is similar in kind (but not extent) to nonlegitimate mourning for people who are defined as not our great concern, such as friends and lovers. That mourning takes place anyway, as the occasional need for therapeutic intervention for bereaved pet owners demonstrates, is a fact of sociological fascination.

SUMMARY

The meanings, grief, bereavement, and mourning involved in the death of pets are similar qualitatively though not usually quantitatively to those involved in the death of people. This is because pets are often seen as humanlike. Human character traits are attributed to pets, and they are often treated in many important respects like family members.

Pets have certain "advantages" over humans in relationships with people. They are less complex, which means that they are never ambivalent, manipulative, argumentative, and so on. They are in a sense like blank slates on which we can inscribe our needs and hopes. They are dependent on us much as children are, but they never "grow up." Because the human character of animals is so clearly a social construction, the study of pets represents a good opportunity to examine that process. Whether in a factual sense they have or don't have these characters, human behavior is often predicated on definition of pets as having human characters.

The death of pets follows the same trajectories as human deaths although euthanasia is much more commonly the outcome. A pet's life often coincides with a period in an owner's life and so comes to symbolize that period. The death of the pet means the end of that period in an owner's life.

The death of a pet disrupts to varying degrees the owner's life. One factor influencing the extent of that disruption is family size. As has been suggested by reactions to human deaths, the larger the family, the less disruptive the death of any one of its members. As long as family size stays small and living alone continues to be a common pattern for single adults and the elderly, pets and consequently their deaths will be significant forces in people's lives.

Grief and bereavement for pets is similar to grief and bereavement for humans. However, in the case of pets, grief is often considered inappropriate and bereavement is often not recognized as legitimate. Because in addition pets sometimes become the objects of displaced grief, the emotional consequences of this failure to legitimate grief for pets can be serious.

Finally, as with grief and bereavement, both public and private mourning for pets resemble mourning for people, but, in addition, are usually stigmatized. The exception is mourning for pet heroes. As with human heroes, these animals are a barometer of the importance of various American values.

In pointing to the similarities between reactions to pet and human deaths, there is no intention of equating the two. To make it seem as though the intensity of grief over animals is usually as severe as for human deaths wildly overstates the case. But to see pet deaths as having little importance and little if any resemblance to human deaths is to make the opposite mistake.

CHAPTER ELEVEN
CHILDREN
AND DEATH

Perhaps the most poignant deaths in contemporary American society are the deaths of children. As Samuel Yudkin (1977:6) expressed it, "Today the death of a child seems an obscenity." This is because of the high value placed on children and also because their deaths are uncommon and, consequently, unexpected. In addition, Americans find it difficult in general to handle death. All children, not simply dying children, who see death shrunk from in fear and disgust are affected by this general American attitude toward death.

This chapter examines both the death attitudes of children and attitudes toward the death of children. To do this, it is necessary first to look at the changing place of the child and the changing demography of death, that is, to situate historically children as a social category and children's deaths.

CHANGES IN THE SOCIAL CONSTRUCTION OF THE CHILD AND THE DEMOGRAPHY OF DEATH

We use our own position historically and culturally as a reference point to understand other times and other places. (These tendencies are called, respectively, *temporocentrism* and *ethnocentrism*.) This is more difficult to do when times and roles are changing. In such periods, comfortable assumptions about the way things and people are and the way we should act are in question. Our own time is precisely such a period in relation to the role of the child.

If we were to look back at children before the past fifteen or so years, the view would be *relatively* unchanged for several hundred years, at least compared to the period preceding that time. The child as a separate social category probably did not exist in Europe before the sixteenth or seventeenth century (Ariès, 1965; Stone, 1965). That meant that in many respects what we call "children" today were seen and treated no differently from adults. They were found in the places in which adults were found (e.g., taverns), wore the same style of clothing (not as copies of adult clothing but simply the same clothing in smaller sizes), and were expected to do many of the same things adults did. In sum, there were infants and adults and nothing in between.

In the American colonies, it is likely that children were differentiated from adults from the first. In colonial New England, "Puritan journals, autobiographies, and histories are filled with specific references to the differences between children and adults" (Stannard, 1977:46). There were even legal distinctions made between "standards of behavior and appropriate punishment for children, postadolescent youths, and adults" (46). In the obsessively moral view of the Puritans, children were both innocent and evil. As were all people in the Puritan view, children were predestined to go to Heaven or Hell, more likely the latter. For all parents knew, their innocent children might have the seeds of evil in them and be headed for eternal damnation.

In addition to these reasons for caution in becoming attached to their children, Puritan parents had to reconcile themselves to the fact that perhaps one-fourth to one-third of their children would die before the age of 10 (Stannard, 1977:55–56). Stannard suggests that this explains the "restraint and even aloofness" (57) that characterized the relationship between parents and their children and also, perhaps, a consequent minimization of grief.

The image of the child and the death rate of children are factors whose relative balance can produce aloofness, as in the case of the Puritans in the seventeenth and eighteenth centuries, or sentimentality as in the case of Americans in the nineteenth century. By that time, particularly during the Victorian era, sentimentality was an overriding feature of the image of the child. In his study of nineteenth-century American diaries, Paul Rosenblatt (1983:70) pointed out that

> The expectation of a relatively high likelihood of death for a young child seemed to have no effect on grief. During the early part of the nineteenth century, when the deaths of infants and young children were particularly common, there was no less grief for infants and young children than during the latter part of the century.

Even with its self-acknowledged limitations (14–15), Rosenblatt's study suggests that there is nothing inevitable about the relationship between death rate and grief felt. The ability of a high death rate to constrain grief is mediated by how the child is seen. This definition of the role of the child is in turn a product of both general cultural attitudes and specific religious and ethnic ideologies.

During the twentieth century in America, the death rate for children has dropped and the regard for children has risen. In 1900, the infant (under 1 year) mortality rate was 162.4/1,000 infants in the U.S. population; by 1950, it had dropped to 33.0 (U.S. Bureau of the Census, 1975:1:60). By 1982, it had dropped even farther to 11.2 (National Center for Health Statistics, 1983:8), although during the next few years the rate rose slightly, due, some contend, to cuts in federal health care programs.

During this century, the regard for children has risen steadily although the role of the child has recently begun to be transformed. Some maintain that the investment of hope and value in children reaches a level that makes it difficult for children to learn that the world is something other than their plaything. In the terms of developmental psychology, children pass into the stage of omnipotence (the period in which children think they can do anything), but never make it out. As Dumont and Foss (1972:45), paraphrasing Charles Wahl (1958:218), expressed it, "the well-loved, non-rejected child in this society has a propensity to retain unconsciously the infantile certainty of his omnipotence." Or in other words, parents cater to a child's every whim and the need to be indulged is habit forming.

In the late 1960s and early 1970s, children had to share the spotlight with the vaguely defined category called "youth." More recently, some have argued, childhood as an age of innocence is fading and is being replaced by a little adulthood. Neal Postman (1982), the most persuasive proponent of this view, has called it "the disappearance of childhood." If this eventually happens and changes our view of children and their deaths, or whether in fact it is more accurate to call the past twenty years the spread of youth into childhood and adulthood (Kamerman, 1975), children are currently highly valued and their deaths are seen as major tragedies. This valuation is clear in reactions to children's suicides. If the suicides of adolescents are seen as tragic, the suicides of children are simply incomprehensible.

To summarize, even if statistics on infant and child mortality indicate how many have died, the role of the child defines in social terms *who* has died and consequently, what people's reactions will be to their deaths.

ATTITUDES TOWARD THE DEATH OF CHILDREN

Reactions to the death of children are the same in kind (qualitatively) but not in degree (quantitatively) as reactions to the deaths of others. Because children are dependent on adults to so great an extent, their deaths tend to provoke in the bereaved more intense self-accusation and guilt.[1]

Miles and Demi (1983–84) found that guilt is a common feature of parental bereavement, particularly what they term *death causation guilt* and *cultural role guilt*. Death causation guilt stems from parents' belief that they caused the child's death either directly or indirectly. Cultural role guilt stems from parents' belief that they didn't fulfill their obligations as parents. The third most common source of guilt, which was found unexpectedly during the study, is *grief guilt*, that is, "guilt related to perceived failure to grieve correctly or to behave appropriately as a grieving parent" (308–309).

Death causation guilt is tied to a time in which the death rate for children is low enough that parents who somehow fail to keep their children alive see themselves as derelict in their responsibilities, that is, a time in which any death is an "accident" and a child's particularly improbable. (Imagine the likelihood of the same level of guilt—not grief—in the face of the high mortality rate during the plague years in fourteenth-century Europe.) Reinforcing this is the American view of the mastery of nature, that is, that somehow something should have been possible to do to ward off death.

The cultural roots of at least two of these three sources of guilt, cultural role guilt and grief guilt, are even more obvious. As discussed in Chapters Six and Seven, the normative turbulence of a period in which traditional mourning rituals are in question and new ones have not yet emerged, provides few guidelines for mourning properly. It is no wonder that parents question whether or not they grieved properly.

Judith Cook (1983b) suggests other factors that influence parental mourning. The death of a child affects mothers and fathers in different ways related to their respective gender roles. Mothers are expected to be emotionally closer to their children. In addition, they often have a greater share in the care of the dying child. Because this prior relationship with the child influences the intensity of bereavement and the course of mourning, Cook found that mothers reported more difficulty than fathers during the first year after the child's death. On the other hand, the constraints of traditional gender roles also made mourning difficult for fathers. Without a clear cultural prescription for proper mourning behavior, people fall back on more clearly defined role prescriptions. So, men may not be expected or allowed to express openly the grief they may feel.

Seen in a slightly different way, if bereavement, Cook (1984) points out, is a role, parents may have different socialization experiences into that role. Because of their greater involvement in raising children in general and in the care of the dying child in particular, mothers undergo a more intense socialization experience. Fathers are in many ways excluded by role and circumstance from participation in raising a child and caring for a dying child. Consequently, they avoid the daily strain of confronting the child's dying. To the extent that this allows them to distance themselves from the dying child, the experience is "anticipatory socialization for the bereaved role in that it prepared them for life without the ill child" (85).

Futterman and Hoffman (1983) in their study of parents of dying children have constructed a model of a typical career pattern of parents mourning in anticipation of the death of their child. Parents pass through five phases. The first is *acknowledgment* "which entails progressive realization of the inevitability of the child's death" (369). Once the reality of impending death developed, *grieving* began. The strength of the grief diminished over the course of the child's dying. *Reconciliation* overlapped and facilitated grieving. In this phase parents worked through the assault on their sense of the "worth of life in general" (373) and recast death into a more acceptable form, for example, "as a religious event or as a release from a life of suffering" (373). *Detachment,* the outcome of anticipatory grief, followed reconciliation. The timing of this phase of the career was crucial. If detachment preceded death by too much, it was accompanied by guilt sometimes reinforced by judgments of hospital staff of parents' "lack of concern, callous behavior, and disinterest" toward the child (375). On the other hand, if dying preceded detachment, parents experienced greater difficulty in adjusting to the death. In *memorialization,* sometimes begun before the actual death, parents distilled certain characteristics of the child, usually positive, which were then solidified into their permanent image of the dead child. To the extent to which anticipatory mourning was successful, *postbereavement mourning* was shorter and less intense.

Although anticipatory mourning may soften postbereavement mourning to an extent, the death of a child is still likely to create enormous difficulties for the entire family. After the child dies, other relationships that were in abeyance must be restored or reconstituted:

> after the child's death, the family that previously was oriented toward the dying child may experience a loss of purpose and direction, which may create feelings of ambiguity about already-strained relationships and further impede attempts to resolve familial conflicts. (Cook, 1984:90)

Parents use a number of *loss rationales* (Glaser and Strauss, 1964), justifications of the death, to manage their grief. In their study of the use of religion to give meaning to a child's death, Cook and Wimberley (1983) describe three which may be called: *reunion, reverence,* and *retribution.* The most frequently used was the notion that the child had gone to heaven where the parent and the dead child would eventually be reunited (reunion).

Another frequent explanation was that the child's death served some religious purpose, for example, as an inspiration for parents to do good works (reverence). As Cook and Wimberley point out, this rationale is tied to the contemporary image of the child. "As a social category assumed to include innocence and purity, it is especially appropriate that a child should serve as an example of religious faith to others" (230).

Finally, a child's death may be construed as a punishment for the sins of the parents (retribution). Although in one sense this explanation hardly seems comforting, "it validates the sense of guilt frequently experienced by survivors regardless of their actual role in an individual's death" (230).

The vagueness in the definition of the bereavement role is a factor in the adjustment not simply of parents, but also of siblings. Judith Cook (1983a) found adjustment problems (e.g., school problems, fear of death) in a fairly high proportion of sibling survivors of children who had died of cancer. Siblings find their status as brother or sister replaced by the status of bereaved sibling (4). However, the role has no clear shape. Cook maintains that difficulties result from the attempt of siblings to play this role that has been imposed on them. To play a role, it is first necessary to role-take, that is, to try on the role by looking at yourself from the point of view of others (Mead, 1934:135–152). But people and circumstances conspire to make role-taking difficult for those siblings. Children are denied access to crucial information, either intentionally (as when parents send them to stay with relatives or lie to them about the gravity of the situation) or as a latent function of hospital rules that prevent them from visiting the dying child or from following the course of dying and reactions of others (e.g., their parents) to it. In sum, "siblings are excluded from anticipatory socialization to the bereaved role and forced to construct their own part in it" (Cook, 1983a:5–6).

After the child's death, Cook points out, grief work may be hampered if parents refuse to discuss the death or "pretend that nothing has happened and that all is well" (6). On the other hand, denial sometimes comes from the sibling in the form of a refusal to talk about or even listen to parents talk about the dead child (22). The vagueness of the bereavement role, the barriers to effective role-taking, and the cultural encouragement of denial all make it difficult for a surviving child to do grief work.

CHILDREN'S ATTITUDES TOWARD DEATH

There are two major approaches to explaining children's understanding of death. The *developmental approach* explains it as the unfolding of a relatively inflexible sequence of maturational stages. This approach has dominated the study of children's attitudes toward death perhaps because psychologists, physicians, and psychiatric social workers have dominated the study of death in general. It has also dominated popular conceptions of the development of children, including their attitudes toward death.

The *experiential approach,* favored by social scientists, sees children's attitudes developing as a result of experiences they have with death and death attitudes, cultural views of death being one major example of these death attitudes.

The two approaches are substantially different. One evidence of this difference is that representatives of each approach, after paying lip service to the possible value of the other, favor their approach to the almost total exclusion of the other. Examples of both approaches will be presented, but, from the theme of this book, the conclusion should be obvious beforehand: the developmental approach describes a typical sequence in the formation of a child's conception of death, a sequence that is the product of culture, history, role, and experience.

The classic example of the developmental approach is the work of the Hungarian psychologist, Maria Nagy (1959). She studied almost four hundred Hungarian children just after World War II. She claimed that children's ideas about death developed in three stages. In the first stage, between the ages of 3 and 5, death is either not recognized as death, that is, it is equated with departing or sleeping, or it is seen as a matter of degree or as only temporary. In the second stage, between ages 5 and 9, death is personified. Death is "someone" who carries people off. Death is understood as final, but "remote from us. As it is remote our death is not inevitable. Only those die whom the death-man catches and carries off. Whoever can get away does not die" (Nagy, 1959:95–96). In the third stage, age 9 and older, death is recognized as final, inevitable, and universal.

Although Nagy allows for some overlap and slight variations in age at the onset of each stage, she claims that in general the stages, their order, and the ages they encompass are invariant and universal.

A good example of the experiential approach is the research of Myra Bluebond-Langner (1974; 1977; 1978) who studied how terminally ill children understand death. In her review of the literature on children's conceptions of death, she catalogs a number of conflicts between what Nagy found and what other studies found.

One study (McIntire, Angle, and Struempler, 1972) pointed out that children as young as 3 have the insights of Nagy's third stage and that American children between 5 and 9 rarely personify death. Lower-class children see violence as the most likely cause of death while middle-class children are more likely to point to illness and old age.

In another study that compared lower-class black children with middle-class white children, Zweig (1983) found a number of significant differences in conceptions of death. For example, black children more often saw aggression as a cause of death, personified death (especially if they had experienced a death in their lives), and evidenced a greater fear of death. While Zweig also found that age was significant in relation to some attitudes (e.g., there was a stronger belief in younger black children in aggression as a cause of death), these were also influenced by differences in experience. Finally, black children less than white believed in the finality of death. "This suggests that the belief in death as a transitory state is related, not to a cognitive understanding of death, but rather to cultural influences" (42), most probably differences in religious beliefs (the black children were Christian and the white children were Jewish).

After establishing that ideas about death were related to experiences, Bluebond-Langner (1977:53–54) focused on terminally ill children whose lives were steeped in hospital experiences with death. She proposed a model for the role career of a dying child in which changes in the kind of information children acquired about their illnesses were paralleled by experiences that altered their images of themselves in relation to death. In the first stage of information acquisition, children learn what they have is a serious illness. They then learn the names of drugs and their side effects. In the third stage, they learn the reasons for the treatments and procedures to which they are being subjected. This is followed by conceptualizing their disease as a series of relapses and remissions, but without death as the outcome. In the final stage, children understand their diseases as series of relapses and remissions that will eventuate in death.

These stages correspond to five "stages" in the development of a self-concept beginning with the realization that they are seriously ill and ending with the realization that they are dying. In the first stage, they recognize that they are seriously ill and, in the second, that although they are seriously ill, they will get better. In the third stage, the child learns that he will always be ill, but may also become relatively better. In the fourth stage, the child realizes that he will never get better. Finally, in the fifth stage, the child realizes that he is dying. This implies a full understanding of death.

Movement from one stage to another is promoted by a series of experiential contingencies. For example, a child moves to stage 2 only after several clinic visits, conversations there with other children with the same illness, and the announcement to the parents that the child is in remission. A child moves to stage 3 only after a relapse has taken place. Only after a few relapses and remissions does a child move to stage 4. The death of another child is the critical experience in moving a child into the fifth stage.

Bluebond-Langner points out that experience, *not age or intelligence,* is crucial to an understanding of death in the children she studied:

There are 3- and 4-year-olds of average intelligence who know more about their prognosis than very intelligent 9-year-olds. The reason for this is that the 9-year-olds may still be in their first remission, have had fewer clinic visits, and have less experience. (1977:54)

All the children in her study, ranging in age from *18 months* to 14 years, eventually realized that they were dying and that death was "final and irreversible" (51–52). That is a powerful argument against adherence to a rigid developmental model of children's understanding of death.

In addition to examining children's conceptions of death, Bluebond-Langner (1978) looked at the role of the dying child by focusing on the awareness contexts (see Chapter Two) coloring the interaction between parents and children. Mutual pretense was by far the most common context, not as much because death was a taboo subject as because this context allowed children to fulfill their role obligations as they understood them. Dying children have no futures. In that, they resemble the old.

> Their worth can only be measured by what they do now, unlike other children, who have time to prove themselves.
> By practicing the rules of mutual pretense, these children keep the parent/child, doctor/patient relationship from breaking down. (Bluebond-Langner, 1978:213)

Mutual pretense allows them to demonstrate to themselves and to others that they are good sons or daughters, good children, and good patients. Reciprocally, it allows those others to be good parents and good physicians and nurses.

It is obvious from this cursory examination of studies of children's conceptions of death that children understand much more about death than many have given them credit for. Failing to recognize the depth of children's understanding is certainly tied to the image of the child as innocent. This misreading of children's understanding is self-serving. As Charles Wahl (1958:222) maintains,

> The classic adult defense against coping with these anxieties in our children is our assertion, maintained even by professional persons, that children cannot conceive of death in *any* form, and, hence, do not need to be reassured about it. One is reminded again of the certainty of a generation ago that the child *has* no sexual feelings, and hence there cannot be a problem about childhood sexuality.

Since Wahl's paper, there has been increasing acknowledgment of the death awareness of children. This parallels the "adultification" of the child. It is another evidence that as the definition of the child changes, the wisdom about death as well as life we are willing to attribute to children changes with it.

SUMMARY

Children's deaths are among the most powerful tragedies in American society because children are so highly valued and because their deaths are relatively uncommon. Changes in the attitudes toward children's death can be seen as an interplay of changes in the role of the child and changes in the demography of children's death. Where many children died and the valuation of children was ambiguous (as in colonial New England), the tragedy of their deaths did not assume the proportions it does today. This is a period when valuation is high and death rate is low.[2] Of the two factors, social valuation is the more important. Because of this, if childhood as we know it (i.e., as the age of innocence) disappears and a greater homogenization of children's and adult's roles follows, it is likely that the tragic power of children's deaths will diminish.

For the moment, however, bereavement for children is marked by great intensity and the salience of guilt. Parental guilt is related to the culturally defined role responsibilities of parents to take care of their children and, after their children's deaths, to grieve properly. The vagueness of the bereavement role offers little guidance for proper grieving.

Culture also intrudes on parental grieving by structuring different bereavement experiences for fathers and mothers, that is, the character of the grief process is tied to gender roles. Cultural mandates for the proper amount of grieving encourage guilt in parents who may have resolved their grief before their children have died. This resolution may be aided by the use of loss rationales.

The vagueness of the bereavement role and other cultural constraints also influence the behavior of siblings. Siblings may be denied access to information about their brother's or sister's dying; this makes it difficult to know what's expected of them.

Children's attitudes toward and conceptions of death are also subject to social and cultural influences. Although the developmental approach to explaining their ideas about death had been popular until recently, studies of the influence of actual experiences with death as well as the influence of socioeconomic, religious, and ethnic factors have made a rigid adherence to the developmental view untenable. Whatever maturational predispositions are thought to lie beneath the surface, the influence of culture, history, role, and experience is obvious and undeniable. In some sense, theories about what children do or don't understand about death reveal as much about the theorists and their age as they do about the children and their ages.

Notes

   1. Of course, old people may also be dependent, but because they are not as highly valued as children, their dependence becomes onerous rather than poignant.
   2. Certainly the reverse is evidenced by attitudes toward the deaths of the elderly.

POSTSCRIPT: DEATH IN THE MIDST OF LIFE

This book is an introduction to the sociological study of dying, death, grief, and mourning. Its major theme has been the necessity of studying death in America in relation to life in America. The meanings of death and dying are constructed out of the values and understandings of American culture. The behaviors relating to dying and mourning are expressions of those meanings and the social arrangements of American society.

Although there has been some movement away from avoidance and denial, these patterns still characterize the response of most Americans to death. It is always important to keep the dimensions of the current situation in mind in discussing the direction of change. It is tempting to see the direction changes are moving in as an already accomplished fact. So we may prefer to see the honest confrontation with death as the existing state of affairs rather than a possible endpoint in the shift, just begun, away from avoidance and denial.

The movement in the scene of dying from homes to institutions has begun to level off, perhaps even to turn in the other direction. Until recently, a continuing increase in the importance of institutions for dying and death seemed almost inevitable. But crowded hospitals and old age homes, insurance coverage for home care of the dying, and growing interest in alternatives to institutions began a shift back to going home to die. Changes in the health care industry and the recent threats to the dominance of medicine also contribute to the shift away from institutions. However, this should not obscure the fact that most people who die in the United States still die in institutions.

In the same way, the deritualization of mourning may obscure the fact that most people still hold traditional funerals and tend to report satisfaction with them. And, of course, change may even reverse its course. The extensive ritual mourning over the deaths in 1986 of the crew of the space shuttle *Challenger* reminded us of the continuing existence of a strong need to engage in ceremonies that express both our confrontation with mortality and our national "consciousness of kind."

There is a reasonable likelihood that quasi-death experiences will grow in importance as they grow in number and as we encounter real deaths later and later in our lives, deaths often robbed of power by anticipatory grief. Quasi-death experiences may more and more become the characteristic occasions for our grief. On the other hand, megadeath in war or environmental catastrophe would sweep this trend away.

As the American population ages, the accumulation of the elderly may change the center of gravity of popular culture and make old age and the association of death with it less stigmatic. The importance of anticipatory grief may continue to grow and numb our sensitivity to the deaths of the elderly. An older population may make youth more and more precious and the deaths of the young that much more shocking.

The meaning of suicide may change with the acceptance of euthanasia. Certainly, the definition of suicide as a social problem is tied to the valuation of the groups who commit suicide, for example, the rise in adolescent suicide eclipsing the higher rate of suicide among the elderly.

The popular interest (as opposed to the serious research interest) in near-death experiences may represent a resurgence in the denial of death, this time in the guise of science. It may grow or return to the scientific obscurity from which it came.

Pets are mirrors that reflect our views of ourselves. Certainly mourning for pets is tied to the economic condition of society as well as to the patterns of mourning for humans. Sentimentality over pets would not likely survive brutalizing catastrophes such as war, environmental calamity, and cataclysmic economic depression.

The significance of the deaths of children is linked to the meaning attached to children in American society. If childhood "disappears," the special poignancy of children's deaths will likely disappear with it. On the other hand, if children become less numerous in an aging society, their special quality and the special quality of their loss may grow in importance.

Finally, the rise in attention to death may be replaced by a falling-off of interest in death. As the Duc de la Rochefoucauld wrote, "One cannot look directly at either the sun or death" (quoted in Dumont and Foss, 1972:33). Perhaps this is true of societies as well as individuals. Certainly, events may conspire to cause a turning away from death. Or, the endless public scrutiny to which death is being subjected may produce a similar effect by trivializing it.

In sum, prophecy is a shaky business at best.

In this postscript, one scientific principle applied throughout the book has already been abandoned: *do not engage in unsupported speculation.* The second, *do not make value judgments,* is about to be. To look at death with relative clarity, it is necessary to abandon the value biases that ordinarily color our outlook on life. But death is laden with powerful feelings of dread. Around it swirl not simply emotions but some of our most important values.

In a paper entitled "Death and the Self," psychologist John P. Brantner (1971) examined the bases for our fear of death. One by one he proposes them, then disposes of them. For example, we are afraid death will "overtake us with projects unfinished, with things undone, and with secrets poorly concealed" (18). We need to realize, he writes, that this is inevitable throughout our lives. We must adjust our goals accordingly. We may fear that dying will be painful. Medicine has to a great extent made that unlikely. We may "fear death because we want to live forever" (19). In a rather cynical way, H. G. Wells, Julian Huxley, and G. P. Wells (1931:1434) set that fear to rest:

> The bad habits he has acquired, the ineradicable memories, the mutilations and distortions that have been his lot, the poison and prejudice and decay in him—are surely all better erased at last and forgotten. A time will come when he will be weary and ready to sleep.
> It is the young who want personal immortality, not the old.

After confronting the bases of our fears of death, Brantner (1971:24–26 passim) offers an assessment of the value of death education. It is also a reaffirmation of life lived in the shadow of death.

> In the fullest and highest sense, the greatest contribution that death education can make to life is, of course, the gift of love. Quite simply, we cannot know life to its fullest without knowing death; hence love itself is intensified and enriched by death.
> Life has many purposes, and we all pursue many goals. But all of these goals and all of these purposes, from the most trivial to the most consummate, are enhanced by the knowledge of our personal finiteness—our time is limited. There are only a limited number of books we can read, a limited number of countries we can visit and explore. We can savor only so many sights and sounds, and we can learn only a limited amount of knowledge and wisdom. What we can accomplish can be measured, and it will be. We must early take measure of our powers, take measure of our own strengths and then, with disability and death before us, establish our own priorities. What will be important to us? We are led to this task sooner and better if we know that death too soon puts a period to all of our strivings and shows us the true worth of all of our possessions.
> It is a very healthy exercise, by the way, to wander through our rooms regularly noting the things that may well have to be disposed of by somebody else someday.
> One of the greatest goals of life is our transformation as organisms to a complete and fully-developed person. This is our central goal: the development of self. And this is accomplished only in relationships with other persons. Here death makes its greatest gift, for the sure and ever-present awareness that I shall die much sooner than I would wish, and that others are moving as quickly and as surely to the same end, enhances all human relationships from that of casual acquaintance to that of deepest love.
> We do not have time for casualness, for thoughtlessness, for selfishness in our relationships with other people. If only we can learn to act as if we are going to die then death loses much of its power over us. Then we can see that we have no time for relationships that detract rather than build, and perhaps we will strive continually against resentment, trivial argument, and all other feelings that drive wedges between us. If we know

that each meeting could be our last, we can strive to lift each relation with another person one notch higher, from stranger to encounter, from casual encounter to acquaintance, from acquaintance to friendship, and from friendship to love. Perhaps we will realize then that each parting from another may well be the final one. Well educated in death, we may then see that the relationships between human beings can transcend not only place, age, distance, and time but also, in the end, transcend even death itself. If we realize that love is stronger than death, we may see that the length of life is not important.

My memory is no longer or shorter than any other man's. It extends from the present moment back to my infancy, and its fullness is not related to my years. This is true as well of the future. I have today, at this moment, only the present. I only have my dreams and my hopes for the future, and no man living has more. We can understand and appreciate life only if we understand and accept death, if we put death in its proper, indeed honorable, place and then get on with living. Perhaps we can begin even to explore again the richness around us and to realize not only our own potential but the potential of life itself.

If we can reconcile the sobriety of living each day as though it were our last with the abandon of living each day as though we had infinite time, we might strike the compromise Brantner suggests and keep life and death in balance.

REFERENCES

142   *REFERENCES*

ALBANO, EDWIN H. 1969. "The Medical Examiner's Viewpoint." Pp. 19–25 in *The Moment of Death: A Symposium,* edited by Arthur Winter. Springfield, Ill.: Charles C Thomas.
ANTHONY, P. D. 1977. *The Ideology of Work.* London: Tavistock.
ARIÈS, PHILIPPE 1965. *Centuries of Childhood: A Social History of Family Life,* translated by Robert Baldick. New York: Vintage.
ARIÈS, PHILIPPE. 1975. "Death Inside Out," translated by Bernard Murchland. Pp. 9–24 in *Death Inside Out: The Hastings Center Report,* edited by Peter Steinfels and Robert M. Veatch. New York: Harper & Row.
ATKINSON, J. MAXWELL. 1971. "Societal Reactions to Suicide: The Role of Coroners' Definitions." Pp. 165–191 in *Images of Deviance,* edited by Stanley Cohen. Baltimore: Penguin.
ATKINSON, J. MAXWELL. 1978. *Discovering Suicide: Studies in The Social Organization of Sudden Death.* Pittsburgh: University of Pittsburgh.
AUDETTE, JOHN R. 1982. "Historical Perspectives on Near-Death Episodes and Experiences." Pp. 21–43 in *A Collection of Near-Death Research Readings,* edited by Craig R. Lundahl. Chicago: Nelson-Hall.
BACKER, BARBARA A., NATALIE HANNON, and NOREEN A. RUSSELL. 1982. *Death and Dying: Individuals and Institutions.* New York: Wiley.
BAKAN, DAVID. 1969. "Suicide and Immortality." Pp. 120–128 in *On the Nature of Suicide,* edited by Edwin S. Shneidman. San Francisco: Jossey-Bass.
BALL, DONALD W. 1971. "Cats & Dogs & People." *Trans-action,* February, pp. 44–47.
BEILIN, ROBERT. 1981–82. "Social Functions of Death." *Omega* 12:25–35.
BENOLIEL, JEANNE QUINT. 1977. "Nurses and the Human Experience of Dying." Pp. 123–142 in *New Meanings of Death,* edited by Herman Feifel. New York: McGraw-Hill.
BERGER, BENNETT M. 1969. "The New Stage of American Man—Almost Endless Adolescence." *The New York Times,* November 2, Sec. 6, pp. 32–33, 131–136.
BERGER, PETER L. and THOMAS LUCKMANN. 1966. *The Social Construction of Reality: A Treatise in the Sociology of Knowledge.* Garden City, N.Y.: Doubleday.
BIKALES, GERDA. 1975. "The Dog as 'Significant Other'." *Social Work* 20:150–152.
BLAU, ZENA SMITH. 1956. "Changes in Status and Age Identification." *American Sociological Review* 21:198–203.
BLAUNER, ROBERT. 1966. "Death and Social Structure." *Psychiatry* 29:378–394.
BLUEBOND-LANGNER, MYRA. 1974. "I Know, Do You? A Study of Awareness, Communication, and Coping in Terminally Ill Children." Pp. 171–181 in *Anticipatory Grief,* edited by Bernard Schoenberg et al. New York: Columbia University Press.
BLUEBOND-LANGNER, MYRA. 1977. "Meanings of Death to Children." Pp. 47–66 in *New Meanings of Death,* edited by Herman Feifel. New York: McGraw-Hill.
BLUEBOND-LANGNER, MYRA. 1978. *The Private Worlds of Dying Children.* Princeton, N.J.: Princeton University Press.
BLUMER, HERBERT. 1969. *Symbolic Interactionism: Perspective and Method.* Englewood Cliffs, N.J.: Prentice-Hall.

BOLDT, MENNO. 1982–83. "Normative Evaluations of Suicide and Death: A Cross-Generational Study." *Omega* 13:145–57.
BOLLEN, KENNETH A. and DAVID P. PHILLIPS. 1982. "Imitative Suicides: A National Study of the Effects of Television News Stories." *American Sociological Review* 47:802–809.
BOWMAN, LEROY. 1959. *The American Funeral.* Washington, D.C.: Public Affairs Press.
BRANTNER, JOHN P. 1971. "Death and the Self." Pp. 15–27 in *Death Education: Preparation for Living,* edited by Betty R. Green and Donald P. Irish. Cambridge, Mass.: Schenkman.
CAMPBELL, THOMAS W., VIRGINIA ABERNETHY, and GLORIA J. WATERHOUSE. 1983–84. "Do Death Attitudes of Nurses and Physicians Differ?" *Omega* 14:43–49.
CARAS, ROGER. 1982. "How to Handle the Death of a Pet." *Ladies Home Journal,* August, p. 78.
CASSELL, ERIC J. 1975. "Dying in a Technological Society." Pp. 43–48 in *Death Inside Out: The Hastings Center Report,* edited by Peter Steinfels and Robert M. Veatch. New York: Harper & Row.
Centers for Disease Control. 1985. *Suicide Surveillance, 1970–1980.* Atlanta: Centers for Disease Control.
CHARMAZ, KATHY CALKINS. 1976. "A Symbolic Interactionist Critique of Kübler-Ross' Stages of Dying." Paper presented at the meetings of the American Sociological Association, New York.
CHARMAZ, KATHY. 1980. *The Social Reality of Death: Death in Contemporary America.* Reading, Mass.: Addison-Wesley.
CLAYTON, PAULA, LYNN DESMARAIS, and GEORGE WINOKUR. 1968. "A Study of Normal Bereavement." *American Journal of Psychiatry* 125:64–74.
COE, RODNEY M. 1978. *Sociology of Medicine,* 2nd ed. New York: McGraw-Hill.
Consumer Union. 1977. *Funerals: Consumers' Last Rights.* New York: Pantheon.
Continental Association of Funeral and Memorial Societies. 1983. *Directory of Member Societies.* Washington, D.C.: Continental Association.
COOK, JUDITH A. 1983a. "The Bereavement of Siblings Following Childhood Deaths." Paper presented at the meetings of the American Sociological Association, Detroit.
COOK, JUDITH A. 1983b. "A Death in the Family: Parental Bereavement in the First Year." *Suicide and Life-Threatening Behavior* 13:42–61.
COOK, JUDITH A. 1984. "Influence of Gender on the Problems of Parents of Fatally Ill Children." *Journal of Psychosocial Oncology* 2:71–91.
COOK, JUDITH A. and DALE W. WIMBERLEY. 1983. "If I Should Die Before I Wake: Religious Commitment and Adjustment to the Death of a Child." *Journal for the Scientific Study of Religion* 22:222–238.
COOMBS, ROBERT H. and PAULINE S. POWERS. 1976. "Socialization for Death: The Physician's Role." Pp. 15–36 in *Toward a Sociology of Death and Dying,* edited by Lyn H. Lofland. Beverly Hills, Calif.: Sage.
CUSACK, ODEAN and ELAINE SMITH. 1984. *Pets and the Elderly. The Therapeutic Bond.* New York: Haworth.
DANIELS, ARLENE KAPLAN. 1973. "How Free Should Professions Be?" Pp. 39–57 in *The Professions and Their Prospects,* edited by Eliot Freidson. Beverly Hills, Calif.: Sage.

DAVIES, CELIA. 1983. "Professionals in Bureaucracies: The Conflict Thesis Revisited." Pp. 177–194 in *The Sociology of Professions: Lawyers, Doctors, and Others,* edited by Robert Dingwall and Philip Lewis. London: Macmillan.

DICKINSON, GEORGE E. 1981. "Death Education in U.S. Medical Schools: 1975–1980." *Journal of Medical Education* 56:111–114.

DICKINSON, GEORGE E. and ALGENE A. PEARSON. 1979a. "Differences in Attitudes Toward Terminal Patients Among Selected Medical Specialties of Physicians." *Medical Care* 17:682–685.

DICKINSON, GEORGE E. and ALGENE A. PEARSON. 1979b. "Sex Differences of Physicians in Relating to Dying Patients." *Journal of the American Medical Women's Association* 34:45–47.

DICKINSON, GEORGE E. and ALGENE A. PEARSON. 1980–81. "Death Education and Physicians' Attitudes Toward Dying Patients." *Omega* 11:167–174.

DOKA, KENNETH J. 1984–85. "Expectation of Death, Participation in Funeral Arrangements, and Grief Adjustment." *Omega* 15:119–129.

DORNETTE, WILLIAM H. L. 1982. "How Does Your State Define Death?" Pp. 119–122 in *Sourcebook on Death and Dying,* edited by James A. Fruehling. Chicago: Marquis.

DOUGLAS, JACK D. 1967. *The Social Meanings of Suicide.* Princeton, N.J.: Princeton University.

DUMONT, MATTHEW P. 1966. "Death of the Leader in a Group of Schizophrenics." *International Journal of Group Psychotherapy* 16:209–216.

DUMONT, RICHARD G. and DENNIS C. FOSS. 1972. *The American View of Death: Acceptance or Denial?* Cambridge, Mass.: Schenkman.

DURKHEIM, EMILE. 1951. *Suicide: A Study in Sociology,* translated by John A. Spaulding and George Simpson. New York: Free Press.

DURKHEIM, EMILE. 1961. *The Elementary Forms of the Religious Life,* translated by Joseph Ward Swain. New York: Collier.

EDDY, JAMES M. and WESLEY J. ALLES. 1983. *Death Education.* St. Louis: Mosby.

ETTINGER, R. C. W. 1966. *The Prospect of Immortality.* New York: McFadden-Bartell.

FAULKNER, ROBERT R. 1973. "Orchestra Interaction: Some Features of Communication and Authority in an Artistic Organization." *Sociological Quarterly* 14:147–157.

FEIFEL, HERMAN, ed. 1959. *The Meaning of Death.* New York: McGraw-Hill.

FEIFEL, HERMAN. 1963. "Death." Pp. 8–21 in *Taboo Topics,* edited by Norman L. Farberow. New York: Atherton.

FEIFEL, HERMAN, ed. 1977. *New Meanings of Death.* New York: McGraw-Hill.

FEIFEL, HERMAN et al. 1967. "Physicians Consider Death." *Proceedings of the 75th Annual Convention of the American Psychological Association* 2:201–202.

FREEMAN, HOWARD E., ORVILLE G. BRIM, JR., and GREER WILLIAMS. 1970. "New Dimensions of Dying." Pp. xiii–xxvi in *The Dying Patient,* edited by Orville G. Brim, Jr., et al. New York: Russell Sage.

FREIDSON, ELIOT. 1970a. *Profession of Medicine: A Study of the Sociology of Applied Knowledge.* New York: Dodd, Mead.

FREIDSON, ELIOT. 1970b. *Professional Dominance: The Structure of Medical Care.* New York: Atherton.

FREIDSON, ELIOT, ed. 1973. *The Professions and Their Prospects.* Beverly Hills, Calif.: Sage.

FREIDSON, ELIOT. 1983. "The Theory of Professions: State of the Art." Pp. 19–37 in *The Sociology of the Professions: Lawyers, Doctors and Others,* edited by Robert Dingwall and Philip Lewis. London: Macmillan.

FUDIN, CAROLE E. and WYNETTA DEVORE. n.d. "The Unidentified Bereaved." Unpublished paper.

FUJII, MASAO. 1983. "Maintenance and Change in Japanese Traditional Funerals and Death-Related Behavior." *Japanese Journal of Religious Studies* 10:39–64.

FULTON, ROBERT. 1971. "Attitudes of People Toward Death, Grief, and the Funeral: An Analysis (1963) of a Study (1962)." Pp. 13–23 in *A Compilation of Studies of Attitudes Toward Death, Funerals, Funeral Directors,* edited by Robert Fulton. n.p.: Robert Fulton.

FULTON, ROBERT, ed. 1965. *Death and Identity.* New York: Wiley.

FULTON, ROBERT, ed. 1976. *Death and Identity.* rev. ed. Bowie, Md.: The Charles Press.

FULTON, ROBERT and JULIE FULTON. 1971. "A Psychological Aspect of Terminal Care: Anticipatory Grief." *Omega* 2:91–99.

FULTON, ROBERT and GILBERT GEIS. 1962. "Death and Social Values." *Indian Journal of Social Research* 3:7–14.

FUTTERMAN, EDWARD H. and IRWIN HOFFMAN. 1983. "Mourning the Fatally Ill Child." Pp. 366–381 in *The Child and Death,* edited by John E. Schowalter et al. New York: Columbia University Press.

GARFIELD, CHARLES A. 1979. "The Dying Patient's Concern with 'Life After Death.'" Pp. 45–60 in *Between Life and Death,* edited by Robert Kastenbaum. New York: Springer.

GIBBS, JACK P. and WALTER T. MARTIN. 1964. *Status Integration and Suicide: A Sociological Study.* Eugene, Ore.: University of Oregon Press.

GLASER, BARNEY G. and ANSELM L. STRAUSS. 1964. "The Social Loss of Dying Patients." *American Journal of Nursing* 64:119–121.

GLASER, BARNEY G. and ANSELM L. STRAUSS. 1965. *Awareness of Dying.* Chicago: Aldine.

GLASER, BARNEY G. and ANSELM L. STRAUSS. 1968. *Time for Dying.* Chicago: Aldine.

GOFFMAN, ERVING. 1961. *Asylums. Essays on the Social Situation of Mental Patients and Other Inmates.* Garden City, N.Y.: Anchor.

GORER, GEOFFREY. 1965. *Death, Grief, and Mourning.* Garden City, N.Y.: Doubleday.

GROSSO, MICHAEL. 1982. "Toward an Explanation of Near-Death Phenomena." Pp. 205–230 in *A Collection of Near-Death Research Readings,* edited by Craig R. Lundahl. Chicago: Nelson-Hall.

GUBRIUM, JABER F. 1976. "Death Worlds in a Nursing Home." Pp. 83–104 in *Toward a Sociology of Death and Dying,* edited by Lyn H. Lofland. Beverly Hills, Calif.: Sage.

GUSTAFSON, ELIZABETH. 1972. "Dying: The Career of the Nursing Home Patient." *Journal of Health and Social Behavior* 13:226–235.

HABENSTEIN, ROBERT W. and WILLIAM M. LAMERS. 1962. *The History of American Funeral Directing,* rev. ed. Milwaukee: Bulfin.

HACKETT, THOMAS P. and AVERY D. WEISMAN. 1964. "Reactions to the Imminence of Death." Pp. 300–311 in *The Threat of Impending Disaster: Contributions to the Psychology of Stress,* edited by George H. Grosser,

Henry Wechsler, and Milton Greenblatt. Cambridge, Mass.: M.I.T. Press.

HALE, RONALD J., RAYMOND L. SCHMITT, and WILBERT M. LEONARD II. 1984. "Social Value of the Age of the Dying Patient: Systematization, Validation, and Direction." *Sociological Focus* 17:157–173.

HARDT, DALE VINCENT. 1978–79. "An Investigation of the Stages of Bereavement." *Omega* 9:279–285.

HENRY, JULES. 1963. *Culture Against Man.* New York: Vintage.

HICKROD, LUCY JEN HUANG and RAYMOND L. SCHMITT. 1982. "A Naturalistic Study of Interaction and Frame: The Pet as 'Family Member'." *Urban Life* 11:55–77.

HOFLING, CHARLES K. et al. 1966. "An Experimental Study in Nurse-Physician Relationships." *Journal of Nervous and Mental Disease* 143:171–180.

HOWARD, ALAN and ROBERT A. SCOTT. 1965–66. "Cultural Values and Attitudes Toward Death." *Journal of Existentialism* 6:161–174.

HUGHES, EVERETT C. 1937. "Institutional Office and the Person." *American Journal of Sociology* 63:404–413.

HUGHES, EVERETT CHERRINGTON. 1958. *Men and Their Work.* New York: Free Press.

HUGHES, EVERETT CHERRINGTON. 1965. "The Study of Occupations." Pp. 442–458 in *Sociology Today: Problems and Prospects,* Vol. II, edited by Robert K. Merton, Leonard Broom, and Leonard S. Cottrell, Jr. New York: Harper & Row.

JONSEN, ALBERT, MARK SIEGLER, and WILLIAM J. WINSLADE. 1982. *Clinical Ethics: A Practical Approach to Ethical Decisions in Clinical Medicine.* New York: Macmillian.

KALISH, RICHARD A. 1981. *Death, Grief, and Caring Relationships.* Monterey, Calif.: Brooks/Cole.

KALISH, RICHARD A. and HELENE GOLDBERG. 1979–80. "Community Attitudes Toward Funeral Directors." *Omega* 10:335–346.

KAMERMAN, JACK. 1975. "Generation and Aging: Baby Steps Toward a Social Psychology with a Sense of History." Paper presented at the meetings of the Society for the Study of Social Problems, San Francisco.

KAMERMAN, JACK. 1984. Review of *A Collection of Near-Death Research Readings,* edited by Craig R. Lundahl. *Contemporary Sociology* 13:120.

KAMERMAN, JACK. 1985. "Quasi-Death and Real-Death Experiences: An Interactionist Approach to the 'Intersections of Biography and History'." Paper presented at the meetings of the Midwest Sociological Society, St. Louis.

KASTENBAUM, ROBERT J. 1981. *Death, Society, and Human Experience,* 2nd ed. St. Louis: Mosby.

KELLY, LUCIE YOUNG. 1981. *Dimensions of Professional Nursing,* 4th ed. New York: Macmillan.

KLAPP, ORRIN E. 1969. *Collective Search for Identity.* New York: Holt, Rinehart and Winston.

KOFF, THEODORE H. 1980. *Hospice: A Caring Community.* Cambridge, Mass.: Winthrop.

KRAUSS, DAVID. 1985. "Beam Me Up, Scotty! Launching the Remains of Your Loved One into Orbit." *The Gazette, Greenwich, Connecticut,* July 4, p. 18.

KÜBLER-ROSS, ELISABETH. 1969. *On Death and Dying.* New York: Macmillan.

KÜBLER-ROSS, ELISABETH. 1970. "The Dying Patient's Point of View." Pp. 156–170 in *The Dying Patient,* edited by Orville G. Brim, Jr., et al. New York: Russell Sage.

LERNER, MONROE. 1970. "When, Why, and Where People Die." Pp. 5–29 in *The Dying Patient,* edited by Orville G. Brim, Jr., et al. New York: Russell Sage.

LEVITON, DANIEL. 1977. "Death Education." Pp. 253–272 in *New Meanings of Death,* edited by Herman Feifel. New York: McGraw-Hill.

LEWIS, LIONEL S. and DENNIS BRISSETT. 1967. "Sex as Work: A Study of Avocational Counseling." *Social Problems* 15:8–17.

LINDEMANN, ERICH. 1944. "Symptomatology and Management of Acute Grief." *American Journal of Psychiatry* 101:141–148.

LINDEMANN, ERICH. 1963. "Grief." Pp. 703–706 in *The Encyclopedia of Mental Health,* Vol. II, edited by Albert Deutsch and Helen Fishman. New York: Franklin Watts.

LOFLAND, LYN H. 1978. *The Craft of Dying: The Modern Face of Death.* Beverly Hills, Calif.: Sage.

LUNDAHL, CRAIG R., ed. 1982. *A Collection of Near-Death Research Readings.* Chicago: Nelson-Hall.

MACDOUGALL, JOHN. 1980. "Changing Physician Ideologies on the Care of the Dying: Themes and Possible Explanations." *Journal of Sociology and Social Welfare* 7:403–424.

MANDELBAUM, DAVID G. 1959. "Social Uses of Funeral Rites." Pp. 189–217 in *The Meaning of Death,* edited by Herman Feifel. New York: McGraw-Hill.

MARIS, RONALD. 1985. "The Adolescent Suicide Problem." *Suicide and Life-Threatening Behavior* 15:91–109.

MARSHALL, VICTOR W. 1975. "Socialization for Impending Death in a Retirement Village." *American Journal of Sociology* 80:1124–1144.

MARSHALL, VICTOR W. 1976. "Organizational Features of Terminal Status Passage in Residential Facilities for the Aged." Pp. 115–134 in *Toward a Sociology of Death and Dying,* edited by Lyn H. Lofland. Beverly Hills, Calif.: Sage.

MARTIN, WALTER T. 1968. "Theories of Variation in the Suicide Rate." Pp. 74–96 in *Suicide,* edited by Jack P. Gibbs. New York: Harper & Row.

MAUKSCH, HANS O. 1975. "The Organizational Context of Dying." Pp. 7–24 in *Death. The Final State of Growth,* edited by Elisabeth Kübler-Ross. Englewood Cliffs, N.J.: Prentice-Hall.

MCBEE, SUSANNA. 1985. "Heroes Are Back. Young Americans Tell Why." *U.S. News & World Report.* April 22, pp. 44–48.

MCINTIRE, M., C. ANGLE, and L. STRUEMPLER. 1972. "The Concept of Death in Midwestern Children and Youth." *American Journal of Diseases of Children* 123:527–532.

MCINTOSH, JOHN L., RICHARD W. HUBBARD, and JOHN F. SANTOS. 1983. "Suicide Facts and Myths: A Compilation and Study of Prevalence." Paper presented at the meetings of the American Association of Suicidology, Dallas.

MCINTOSH, JOHN L. and BARBARA L. JEWELL. 1986. "Sex Difference Trends in Completed Suicide." *Suicide and Life-Threatening Behavior* 16:16–27.

MEAD, GEORGE HERBERT. 1932. *The Philosophy of the Present.* Chicago: University of Chicago.

MEAD, GEORGE HERBERT. 1934. *Mind, Self, and Society: From the Stand-*

point of a Social Behaviorist, edited by Charles W. Morris. Chicago: University of Chicago.

MEAD, GEORGE HERBERT. 1938. *The Philosophy of the Act.* Chicago: University of Chicago.

MERCY, JAMES A. et al. 1984. "Patterns of Youth Suicide in the United States." *Educational Horizons* 62:124–127.

MILES, MARGARET SHANDOR and ALICE STERNER DEMI. 1983–84."Toward a Theory of Bereavement Guilt: Sources of Guilt in Bereaved Parents." *Omega* 14:299–314.

MILLER, H. L. et al. 1984. "An Analysis of the Effects of Suicide Prevention Facilities on Suicide Rates in the United States." *American Journal of Public Health* 74:340–343.

MILLS, C. WRIGHT. 1959. *The Sociological Imagination.* New York: Oxford.

MITFORD, JESSICA. 1963. *The American Way of Death.* New York: Simon & Schuster.

MITFORD, JESSICA. 1980. "Bake and Shake." *New York,* January 21, pp. 50–52.

MOODY, RAYMOND A., JR. 1976. *Life After Life.* New York: Bantam.

MOODY, RAYMOND A., JR. 1978. *Reflections on Life After Life.* New York: Bantam.

MOR, VINCENT and JEFFREY HIRIS. 1983. "Determinants of Site of Death Among Hospice Cancer Patients." *Journal of Health and Social Behavior* 24:375–385.

MROZEK, SLAWOMIR. 1968. *Tango,* translated by Ralph Manheim and Teresa Dzieduscycka. New York: Grove.

MUMMA, CHRISTINE M. and JEANNE QUINT BENOLIEL. 1984–85. "Care, Cure, and Hospital Dying Trajectories." *Omega* 15:275–288.

NAGY, MARIA H. 1959. "The Child's View of Death." Pp. 79–98 in *The Meaning of Death,* edited by Herman Feifel. New York: McGraw-Hill.

National Center for Health Statistics. 1983. *Annual Summary of Births, Deaths, Marriages, and Divorces: United States, 1982.* Hyattsville, Md.: U.S. Department of Health and Human Services.

National Center for Health Statistics. 1984. *Advance Report of Final Mortality Statistics, 1982.* Hyattsville, Md.: U.S. Department of Health and Human Services.

Newsday. 1982. "Dear Kidsday." *Newsday,* June 20, Kidsday section, n.p.

New York City Board of Education. 1984. *Agreement Between the Board of Education and the United Federation of Teachers Covering Paraprofessionals.* New York: New York City Board of Education.

NOYES, RUSSELL, JR. and ROY KLETTI. 1976. "Depersonalisation in the Face of Life-Threatening Danger: A Description." *Psychiatry* 39:19–27.

OSIS, KARLIS and ERLENDUR HARALDSSON. 1977. "Deathbed Observations by Physicians and Nurses: A Cross-Cultural Survey." *Journal of the American Society of Psychical Research* 71:237–259.

PARSONS, TALCOTT and VICTOR LIDZ. 1967. "Death in American Society." Pp. 133–170 in *Essays in Self-Destruction,* edited by Edwin Shneidman. New York: Science House.

PHILLIPS, DAVID P. 1974. "The Influence of Suggestion on Suicide: Substantive and Theoretical Implications of the Werther Effect." *American Sociological Review* 39:340–354.

PINE, VANDERLYN R. and DEREK PHILLIPS. 1970. "The Cost of Dying: A Sociological Analysis of Funeral Expenditures." *Social Problems* 17:405–417.

POSTMAN, NEIL. 1982. *The Disappearance of Childhood.* New York: Delacorte.
PRATT, LOIS. 1981. "Business Temporal Norms and Bereavement Behavior." *American Sociological Review* 46:317–333.
QUACKENBUSH, JAMES E. 1981. "Pets, Owners, Problems, and the Veterinarian: Applied Social Work in a Veterinary Teaching Hospital." *The Compendium on Continuing Education* 3:764–770.
QUACKENBUSH, JAMES E. 1982. "The Social Context of Pet Loss." *Animal Health Technician* 3:333–337.
QUACKENBUSH, JAMES E. 1984. "Pet Bereavement in Older Owners." Pp. 292–299 in *The Pet Connection,* edited by Robert K. Anderson, Benjamin L. Hart, and Lynette A. Hart. Minneapolis: Center to Study Human-Animal Relationships and Environments.
QUACKENBUSH, JAMIE. 1985. "The Death of a Pet: How It Can Affect Owners." *Veterinary Clinics of North America: Small Animal Practice* 15:395–402.
QUACKENBUSH, JAMES and LAWRENCE GLICKMAN. 1983. "Social Work Services for Bereaved Pet Owners: A Retrospective Case Study in a Veterinary Teaching Hospital." Pp. 377–389 in *New Perspectives on Our Lives with Companion Animals,* edited by A. H. Katcher and A. M. Beck. Philadelphia, University of Pennsylvania Press.
QUACKENBUSH, JAMES E. and LAWRENCE GLICKMAN. 1984. "Helping People Adjust to the Death of a Pet." *Health and Social Work* 9:42–48.
RABIN, DAVID L. and LAUREL H. RABIN. 1970. "Consequences of Death for Physicians, Nurses, and Hospitals." Pp. 171–190 in *The Dying Patient,* edited by Orville G. Brim, Jr., et al. New York: Russell Sage.
RANK, STEVEN G. and CARDELL K. JACOBSON. 1977. "Hospital Nurses' Compliance with Medication Overdose Orders: A Failure to Replicate." *Journal of Health and Social Behavior* 18:188–193.
REA, M. PRISCILLA, SHIRLEY GREENSPAN, and BERNARD SPILKA. 1975. "Physicians and the Terminal Patient: Some Selected Attitudes and Behavior." *Omega* 6:291–305.
RENSBERGER, BOYCE. 1978. *The Cult of the Wild.* Garden City, N.Y.: Anchor.
RING, KENNETH. 1980. *Life at Death: A Scientific Investigation of the Near-Death Experience.* New York: Coward, McCann & Geoghegan.
RING, KENNETH. 1982. "Frequency and Stages of the Prototypic Near-Death Experience." Pp. 110–147 in *A Collection of Near-Death Research Readings,* edited by Craig R. Lundahl. Chicago: Nelson-Hall.
RING, KENNETH and STEPHEN FRANKLIN. 1981–82. "Do Suicide Survivors Report Near-Death Experiences?" *Omega* 12:191–208.
ROSENBLATT, PAUL C. 1983. *Bitter, Bitter Tears: Nineteenth-Century Diarists and Twentieth-Century Grief Theories.* Minneapolis: University of Minnesota Press.
ROTH, JULIUS A. 1963. *Timetables: Structuring the Passage of Time in Hospital Treatment and Other Careers.* Indianapolis: Bobbs-Merrill.
SABOM, MICHAEL B. and SARAH S. KREUTZIGER. 1982. "Physicians Evaluate the Near-Death Experience." Pp. 148–159 in *A Collection of Near-Death Research Readings,* edited by Craig R. Lundahl. Chicago: Nelson-Hall.
SAUNDERS, CICELY. 1977. "Dying They Live: St. Christopher's Hospice." Pp. 153–179 in *New Meanings of Death,* edited by Herman Feifel. New York: McGraw-Hill.

SCHMITT, RAYMOND L. 1982–83. "Symbolic Immortality in Ordinary Contexts: Impediments to the Nuclear Era." *Omega* 13:95–116.
SCHULMAN, SAM. 1979. "Mother Surrogate—After a Decade." Pp. 272–280 in *Patients, Physicians, and Illness: A Sourcebook in Behavioral Science and Health,* 3rd ed., edited by E. Gartly Jaco. New York: Free Press.
SCHULZ, RICHARD and DAVID ADERMAN. 1978–79. "Physicians' Death Anxiety and Patient Outcomes." *Omega* 9:327–332.
SCHUR, EDWIN. 1976. *The Awareness Trap: Self-Absorption Instead of Social Change.* New York: McGraw-Hill.
SEGERBERG, OSBORN, JR. 1974. *The Immortality Factor.* New York: Dutton.
SHEATSLEY, PAUL B. and JACOB J. FELDMAN. 1964. "The Assassination of President Kennedy: A Preliminary Report on Public Reactions and Behavior." *Public Opinion Quarterly* 28:189–215.
SHNEIDMAN, EDWIN S. 1973. *Deaths of Man.* New York: Quadrangle.
SHNEIDMAN, EDWIN S., ed. 1984. *Death: Current Perspectives.* 3rd ed. Palo Alto, Calif.: Mayfield.
SHNEIDMAN, EDWIN. 1985. *Definition of Suicide.* New York: Wiley.
SHOSTAKOVICH, DMITRI. 1979. *Testimony: The Memoirs of Dmitri Shostakovich,* edited by Solomon Volkov and translated by Antonina W. Bouis. New York: Harper & Row.
SILVER, MAURY and DANIEL GELLER. 1978. "On the Irrelevance of Evil: The Organization and Individual Action." *Journal of Social Issues* 34:125–136.
SKOLNICK, JEROME H. 1975. *Justice Without Trial: Law Enforcement in Democratic Society,* 2nd ed. New York: Wiley.
SMITH, HARVEY L. 1955. "Two Lines of Authority Are One Too Many." *Modern Hospital* 84:59–64.
SPIEGEL, JOHN P. 1964. "Cultural Variations in Attitudes Toward Death and Disease. Pp. 283–299 in *The Threat of Impending Disaster: Contributions to the Psychology of Stress,* edited by George Grosser, Henry Wechsler, and Milton Greenblatt. Cambridge, Mass.: M.I.T. Press.
STAFFORD, MARK C. and JACK P. GIBBS. 1985. "A Major Problem with the Theory of Status Integration and Suicide." *Social Forces* 63:643–660.
STANNARD, DAVID E. 1977. *The Puritan Way of Death: A Study in Religion, Culture, and Social Change.* New York: Oxford.
STONE, GREGORY P. 1965. "The Play of Little Children." *Quest* 4:23–31.
STONE, GREGORY P. and HARVEY A. FARBERMAN, eds. 1970. *Social Psychology Through Symbolic Interaction.* Waltham, Mass.: Ginn-Blaisdell.
STONE, GREGORY P. and HARVEY A. FARBERMAN, eds. 1981. *Social Psychology Through Symbolic Interaction,* 2nd ed. New York: Wiley.
STRAUSS, ANSELM L. 1969. *Mirrors and Masks: The Search for Identity.* San Francisco: The Sociology Press.
STRAUSS, ANSELM and BARNEY G. GLASER. 1970a. "Patterns of Dying." Pp. 129–155 in *The Dying Patient,* edited by Orville G. Brim, Jr., et al. New York: Russell Sage.
STRAUSS, ANSELM L. and BARNEY G. GLASER. 1970b. *Anguish: A Case History of a Dying Trajectory.* San Francisco: The Sociology Press.
STRAUSS, ANSELM L. and JEANNE C. QUINT. 1964. "The Nonaccountability of Terminal Care." *Hospitals* 38:73–87.
SUDNOW, DAVID. 1967a. *Passing On: The Social Organization of Dying.* Englewood Cliffs, N.J.: Prentice-Hall.
SUDNOW, DAVID. 1967b. "Dead on Arrival." *Trans-action,* November, pp. 36–43.

SUDNOW, DAVID. 1970. "Dying in a Public Hospital." Pp. 191–208 in *The Dying Patient*, edited by Orville C. Brim, Jr., et al. New York: Russell Sage.

THOMAS, L. EUGENE, PAMELA E. COOPER, and DAVID J. SUSCOVICH. 1982–83. "Incidence of Near-Death and Intense Spiritual Experiences in an Intergenerational Sample: An Interpretation." *Omega* 13:35–41.

THOMAS, WILLIAM I. and DOROTHY SWAINE THOMAS. 1928. *The Child in America: Behavior Problems and Programs*. New York: Knopf.

TIME. 1947. "War Crimes. Subject: Women." *Time*, November 24, p. 33.

TOPOL, PHYLLIS and MARVIN REZNIKOFF. 1982. "Perceived Peer and Family Relationships, Hopelessness, and Locus of Control as Factors in Adolescent Suicide Attempts." *Suicide and Life-Threatening Behavior* 12:141–150.

TOYE, FRANCIS. 1946. *Giuseppe Verdi: His Life and Works*. New York: Knopf.

U.S. Bureau of the Census. 1975. *Historical Statistics of the United States, Colonial Times to 1970, Bicentennial Edition*, 2 vols. Washington, D.C.: U.S. Government Printing Office.

U.S. Bureau of the Census. 1984. *Statistical Abstract of the United States: 1985*. Washington, D.C.: U.S. Government Printing Office.

VERNON, GLENN M. 1970. *Sociology of Death: An Analysis of Death-Related Behavior*. New York: Ronald Press.

VOLKART, EDMUND H. and STANLEY T. MICHAEL. 1957. "Bereavement and Mental Health." Pp. 281–307 in *Explorations in Social Psychiatry*, edited by Alexander H. Leighton, John A. Clausen, and Robert W. Wilson. New York: Basic Books.

WAHL, CHARLES W. 1958. "The Fear of Death." *Bulletin of the Menninger Clinic* 22:214–223.

WALLIS, CHARLES L. 1973. *American Epitaphs: Grave and Humorous*. New York: Dover.

WARNER, W. LLOYD. 1962. *American Life: Dream and Reality*, rev. ed. Chicago: University of Chicago Press.

WASSERMAN, IRA M. 1984. "Imitation and Suicide: A Reexamination of the Werther Effect." *American Sociological Review* 49:427–436.

WEBER, MAX. 1958a. *From Max Weber: Essays in Sociology*, translated by H. H. Gerth and C. Wright Mills. New York: Oxford.

WEBER, MAX. 1958b. *The Protestant Ethic and the Spirit of Capitalism*, translated by Talcott Parsons. New York: Scribner's.

WEISMAN, AVERY D. 1972. *On Dying and Denying: A Psychiatric Study of Terminality*. New York: Behavioral Publications.

WEISMAN, AVERY D. 1977. "The Psychiatrist and the Inexorable." Pp. 107–122 in *New Meanings of Death*, edited by Herman Feifel. New York: McGraw-Hill.

WEISMAN, AVERY D. and THOMAS P. HACKETT. 1961. "Predilection to Death." *Psychosomatic Medicine* 23:232–256.

WELLS, H. G., JULIAN S. HUXLEY, and G. P. WELLS 1931. *The Science of Life*, 2 vols. Garden City, N.Y.: Doubleday, Doran.

WHITLOW, JOAN. 1982. "Nurses and Paramedics Granted Authority to Officially Pronounce Death." *Newark Star-Ledger*, March 11, p. 34.

WILLIAMS, ROBIN M. 1960. *American Society: A Sociological Interpretation*, 2nd ed. New York: Knopf.

WILSON, ROBERT N. 1970. *The Sociology of Health: An Introduction*. New York: Random House.

YUDKIN, SIMON. 1977. "Death and the Young." Pp. 4–13 in *When Children Die*, edited by Loren Wilkenfeld. Dubuque, Iowa: Kendall-Hunt.

ZBOROWSKI, MARK. 1952. "Cultural Components in Responses to Pain." *Journal of Social Issues* 8:16–30.

ZOLA, IRVING KENNETH and STEPHEN J. MILLER. 1973. "The Erosion of Medicine from Within." Pp. 153–172 in *The Professions and Their Prospects*, edited by Eliot Freidson. Beverly Hills, Calif.: Sage.

ZWEIG, APRIL R. 1983. "Children's Attitudes Toward Death." Pp. 36–48 in *The Child and Death*, edited by John E. Schowalter et al. New York: Columbia University Press.

INDEX

NAMES

Abernethy, V., 62
Aderman, D., 59
Albano, E., 19
Alles, W., 30
Angle, C., 130
Anthony, P., 32
Aries, P., 27, 124
Atkinson, J., 90–93, 95

Backer, B., 51
Bakan, D., 100
Ball, D., 112–113
Beilin, R., 38
Benoliol, J., 46, 63
  See also Quint, J.
Berger, B., 97
Berger, P., 22
Bikales, G., 113
Blau, Z., 72
Blauner, R., 8–9, 76, 78
Bluebond-Langner, M., 130–132
Blumer, H., 22
Boldt, M., 98–99, 107
Bollen, K., 98
Bowman, L., 81
Brantner, J., 10, 16, 137–139
Brim, O., 4–5, 11
Brissett, D., 32–33

Campbell, T., 62
Caras, R., 116–120
Cassell, E., 26, 34
Charmaz, K., 6, 11, 28, 32, 42–43,
  67–68, 70, 90, 94
Clayton, P., 67
Coe, R., 53
Coombs, R., 60–61
Cook, J., 127–129
Cooper, P., 105
Cusack, O., 116

Daniels, A., 56
Davies, C., 53
Demi, A., 67
Desmarais, L., 67
Devore, W., 69, 118
Dickinson, G., 43, 59, 64
Doka, K., 80
Dornette, W., 19
Douglas, J., 90, 92, 94
Dumont, R., 28–29, 38, 85, 126, 136
Durkheim, E., 83, 90–92, 94

Eddy, J., 30
Ettinger, R., 34

Farberman, H., 14, 112
Faulkner, R., 53
Feifel, H., 6–7, 27, 58–59
Feldman, J., 83
Fields, W. C., 29
Foss, D., 28–29, 38, 126, 136
Franklin, S., 102, 107
Freeman, H., 4–5, 11
Freidson, E., 47–49, 56–58, 60
Fudin, C., 69, 118
Fujii, M., 81
Fulton, J., 9, 41, 69–71, 82, 86
Fulton, R., 3–4, 6–9, 11, 26, 28,
  31–32, 41, 44, 69–71,
  78–79, 82, 86
Futterman, E., 127–128

Garfield, C., 104
Geis, G., 26
Geller, D., 60
Geller, G., 26
Gibbs, J., 91–92
Glaser, B., 16–17, 22, 26, 32, 36,
  40–41, 47–48, 50, 128
Glickman, L., 116–118, 120

SUBJECTS

Funerals:
changes in, 78–82
costs, 77–78
functions, 76–78
rationalization, 8, 80–81

Goethe, Johann Wolfgang von, 98
Grief:
anticipatory, 9, 41, 70–71
culture and, 69–71, 76–77, 126–127
definition, 66
delayed, 85, 117
guilt, 66–67, 69, 115, 126–127
and identity, 68–72
patterns, 67–69, 86–87, 126–128
symptoms of normal, 66–69
See also Quasi-death experiences; Pets; Children
Grief work, 66–67, 76, 82
Guilt: *see* Grief, guilt

"Happy death movement," 30–31
Hartsdale Canine Cemetery, 119–120
Heim, Albert, 108
Hospices, 51–52
Hospitals, 46–50
Houdini, Harry, 85

I. G. Farben Chemical Trust, 29
Immortality, 100, 102–103

Johnson, Lyndon, 83

Kennedy, John F., 83, 85

Loss:
for nurses, 36
See also Bereavement; Quasi-death experiences
Loss rationales, 128

Megadeath, 5–6
Memorial societies, 31, 79–80
Mourning:
deritualization of, 8, 79–80, 136
effect of business temporal norms on, 80–81
for public figures, 82–85
private, 86–87
public, 76–85
See also Funerals
Mourning dress, 2–3
Mummification, 29, 86

Near-death experiences:
culture and, 104
definition, 102
depersonalization: *see* Depersonalization
effects, 106–108
ethical issues, 107
explanations, 105–106
out-of-body experiences, 103, 106
popularity, 108–110
social construction, 102, 104–106
stages, 103–105
and suicide, 107
Nuclear threat: *see* Megadeath
Nurses:
attitudes toward death, 62–63
behavior with the dying, 16, 35, 47
impact of patient's death on, 36
professional ideology, 43, 57